MW00879468

Table of Contents

This recollection of the events of my life is dedicated to those who gave so much but have never heard the words "Welcome Home".

~Semper Fi~

Mike I. Neil

Brigadier General

USMC

FOREWORD

To the readers of this work:

It is my duty to tell you of the man that Mike Neil is and the value of this book not only as a record of his life but as a reminder to 'Welcome Home' our fellow Vietnam veterans who have been ignored for so long. It is then your job to read the work and decide about the man yourself. I think you will agree with my conclusion that Mike is a man of honorable character and that the nation should be grateful for his years of service.

Not only did Mike distinguish himself through his service in the Marine Corps but in the years after his service in the civilian world during his career as a lawyer.

His career as a combat officer in the Marine Corps is legendary, as attested to by his being a recipient of the Navy Cross for his actions on one particularly chaotic night in the hills of Vietnam.

While Mike and I both served with honors in Vietnam we never actually served in the same unit in that theater of combat. I did however have the pleasure of serving alongside Mike when he was Commanding General of MCB Camp Pendleton during Operations Desert Shield

and Desert Storm. During that time, I was Assistant
Deputy Commandant of the 4th Marine Division. Mike
was a valuable asset to me as I helped the Marine Corps
develop a new Desert Warfare Training Program.

Mike inspired me as I watched his dedication and
professionalism in caring and preparing Marines to go
into combat, as well as taking care of their families. Later
I watched him serve as the Commanding General of the
4th Marine Division. Mike again proved that he was an
accomplished leader with special insights regarding
caring for and preparing Marines for combat. Mike is and
will always be Semper Fi.

Jim. E. Livingston

Major General

USMC

CHAPTER 1
Applause For A Death

    50 caliber rounds make a quite
unmistakable sound. If you have ever heard
them, you will, for the rest of your life, know
the report that they make. For me and the
many like me who have seen combat action,
it is also one of the many sounds you hear
when you close your eyes to sleep at night.

Seeing the helicopter get pelted and listening to the all too familiar echoes of the 50 Cal strangely took me back to my youth. My father was a Marine, and I spent most of my time as a kid on Marine Corps bases around the world. So, I knew the sounds of war before I ever set foot on a battlefield.

The speed with which the rounds smashed into the helicopter was made even more vivid in the film by the tracer rounds linked in with the belt of ammunition. Every fifth round of the four-to- one tracer belt left its red track of magnesium burning hot as it slammed into the metal of the downed helicopter. The rounds worked their way along the side of the downed helicopter until they found a new purchase in the flesh of a young blonde haired American soldier as he tragically tried to climb out of the side door of the aircraft to a safer vantage point away from the now burning fuselage.

The helicopter, which now lay flat on its side in an open rice paddy, was already ripped to pieces from enduring its fall from the sky and promptly took the brunt of the 50 caliber rounds as the young man struggled to

10

make it to safety. Another burst of shots released from the Vietnamese position finally struck him in the chest, with the force of an oncoming truck, sending him backward into the muddy waters of the rice paddy in an awkward twisting ballet of blood and mud. His one-sided struggle against his foe ended with him face down in that rice paddy clinging to life drowning in a combination of his own blood and dirty paddy water. For me, it was the beginning of something much bigger and the reason for this book.

My name is Mike Neil. I am a retired Brigadier General of the United States Marine Corps. I served my country proudly for 24 years as an officer in the Marine Corps, and I can say with pride that I would gladly answer the call of duty again if my country needed me.

To truly understand my story, I will need you to do a few things for me if you will. First, remember the account above because we will come back to it later and in it, you will see everything I have stood for my entire life, all the basic principles of the man I am at my core. Second, I need you to take a journey with me back to my beginnings and then along the path that brought me to how I became the man I am today.

So, I would ask that you lend me your ear and a few short hours of your time as I take you back to what nowadays would be called, an origin story. Maybe then you will be able to see how I not only became who I am but how I left behind some of the better parts of who I was and how after many years I was able to reclaim some of those parts and let go of some of the demons I picked up along the way.

It all started in California! Sunshine, sand, and surf. If there is one real truth in my life that has been there since I was a kid, it is that I love California more than any place on earth, in particular, San Diego, for many reasons, family, friends, the natural beauty and yes, the sunshine. But California, like all places, has dark and overcast days too (albeit few and far between sometimes) and let's be honest if it weren't for the dark days, we wouldn't really have a genuine appreciation for the days filled with sunshine at all.

This is my story, and yes it has some pretty dark days. Days I honestly don't care to remember but couldn't possibly forget if I tried. It seems though, however odd, that it is the darkness of those days that helps me to appreciate the actual rays of sunshine in my life. My family, my friends, my community, my country, and my Corps.

It was the fall of 1965 in Berkeley California, and I was a third-year law student at the University of California Berkeley School of Law. Now if you have never been to California, it is one of the most fabulous places on earth and although Berkley was not quite as sunny as San Diego. For a young man in college, it still meant girls and I was not one to stay inside and study any longer than I had to. I wanted to be outside chasing girls and hanging out with my friends. But between my job, studying and my classes I had little time for much else so girls would have to wait for the time being.

Berkeley is a picturesque campus, and I walked almost everywhere I went in those days. I had a car; yes, but how was I going to meet girls and pay attention to the road at the same time? So, I walked…a lot!

One day while walking up Telegraph Avenue in my third year, I saw a poster stapled to a telephone pole advertising a film about the Viet Cong. The event was being put on by the Young Socialists Alliance at a campus auditorium, and I decided that I would go check it out to hopefully answer some questions I had been asking myself.

You see I had been watching a lot of TV about the Viet Cong recently and had developed a great interest in the American deployment in Southeast Asia and I really wanted to see the opinions of all sides of the conflict so I could make an informed decision on where I stood personally on the subject. I should state here what it seems like a commonly known fact to most, America was heavily divided when it came to our military efforts in Vietnam. But what has never been widely reported was that even though college campuses across America were hot spots for the anti-war effort, many of us supported our soldiers on those campuses as well.

When I arrived at the event that evening, I was obviously out of place with my short hair and shined shoes. I definitely stood out in the crowd, to say the least. A group which was made up mostly of hippy leftists, long-haired students and many nonstudents who made it quite apparent that they had a favorable view of the Viet Cong.

The movie at first showed images of the Viet Cong helping villagers, distributing toothbrushes, health care supplies, food and the like and was honestly just your basic level propaganda film.

Then it turned into something much darker than I could have ever imagined. Something I told you we would come back to just a while ago and asked that you remember, but most likely you have already forgotten. Truth is, I wish I could forget it as well. Hell, I wish I had never seen the damn film to begin with, but sadly it is something that is so boldly emblazoned in my brain that I will always remember the impact each frame of that film had upon my life.

The film progressed from the Viet Cong helping locals to the flight of a Bell UH-1

Iroquois better known as a "Huey" helicopter flying overhead. The Huey was suddenly being riddled with bullets from that 50-caliber machine gun. The unmistakable sound that somehow Marines come to both love and hate simultaneously.

So many rounds hit home that the Huey lost its flight capability and rotated into the rice paddy below ripping off the blades and leaving the fuselage lying on its side motionless except for the repeated impact of the 50 caliber rounds. Slowly a young blonde-haired American soldier, bloody and clinging to life from the crash, climbed out of the side door of the Huey trying to escape certain death inside, knowing his chances outside were only slightly higher. Now you may be asking yourself. Why is he mentioning this again? He just told us this part of the story a few pages ago. I repeat it because this moment, as the crowd's laughter roared at the death of this young soldier, became one of the defining moments of my life.

You see when you reach a certain age, and you look back on your life as a whole, you can see very clearly from the cliff tops of age and experience. What you see is that there are just a few moments that carve out who we really are at our very core. Just a few moments make our morality, honor, and dignity what it will become for the rest of our lives. Watching that young American soldier get ripped to pieces by 50-caliber machine gun rounds was one of those moments for me.

I am not sure if it was the bullets ripping through his flesh and watching him die in what seemed like a slow-motion blur of real life and projected film. Or it was the fact that the majority of the audience cheered, clapped and even stomped their feet in unison as the young soldier bled to death face down in the muddy waters of that rice paddy.

I was speechless. Shocked to my very core and tears flooded my eyes. Tears of both sadness for the dying soldier and rage for those laughing at his death. Tears continued to flow as I walked home from the film, and I can still feel on my face to this day. This was one time I wish I would have driven.

The very next morning I drove over to San Francisco. I quickly found the Marine Corps recruiting office, walked right in, and loudly announced: "I want to become a Marine Corps officer." I had a few caveats to my inductions to the Marine Corps of course not wanting to throw away all my hard work and the recruiter, Captain Larsen, told me that they would not be an issue at all.

First, I wanted to ensure that I would be an infantry officer and not a legal beagle. Second, I needed to finish my school year and take the bar exam before I actually went to begin my Marine training.

Captain Larsen assured me again that none of this would be an issue as long as I could meet the testing requirements which I knew would not be an issue at all for me. I was whip-smart and in the best shape of my life, ready to become a Marine. It was October of 1965 when I completed all of the testing necessary for the Marine Corps and took the "Oath of Office" that all officers take.

The Oath of Office

I (name) do solemnly swear (or affirm)
that I will support and defend the
constitution of the United States against all
enemies foreign and domestic; that I will
bear true faith and allegiance to the same;
that I take this obligation freely; and
without any mental reservation or purpose
of evasion; that I will well and faithfully
discharge the duties of the office on which I
am about to enter; So, help me God.

It is important to me that you know this
Oath of Office (Title 5 U.S. Code 3331),
given to all military officers as well as
elected officials in the United States, and the
oath taken by enlisted soldiers are quite
different. And that there are well thought out
constitutional reasons why. These differences
will come to light later in this book and play
a significant part in our great American
democracy every day by helping bolster a

19

system of checks and balances essential to your great nation.

I then returned to my law school completing my third year of studies, while working 34 hours a week, at three separate jobs. I of course was very active at the time and worked out pretty much every day and from time to time even worked out with the boxing team, even competing in the intramural bouts my third year. I would end up finishing in the top 25 percent of my class, just barely, but still top 25 percent. Which I thought was pretty good since I was working so much and knew that I would be heading to the Marine Corps and most likely war very soon. I spent some time studying for the bar exam (and maybe chasing a girl or two) which I took in July of 1966.

Everyday thoughts of that night I watched that film and that young blonde American soldier dying alone in the muddy water of that rice paddy riddled with 50 caliber bullets and the hundreds of other young men just like him raced through my head. Stamped indelibly on my soul. I could not forget the laughter and cheering that still echoes in my head today.

The fact that my father was a retired Marine had very little to do with my decision to join the Marine Corps, other than the fact that if I were going to go into the military, it would be as a United States Marine Corps officer. Really, I just wanted to do my patriotic duty, like thousands of other young men I was soon to join in Quantico, Virginia for Officers Candidate School and later on the field of battle in Vietnam.

I was due to report to Officers Candidate School in Quantico on October 15, 1966. I had some time and wanted to see the America I loved so much up close, I decided to make the drive across the country in my Volkswagen bug. Which unfortunately was without a radio and left me with only my thoughts as I drove. The journey was lonely, especially Texas, which seemed as if it would never end. I thought about the events of the last year that led me to make my decision to join the Marine Corps as an infantry officer. I thought about my father, my family, the girls that I fancied but mostly about that young soldier dying alone on the field of battle and how I would deal with that sort of situation if it were me. Because honestly, that possibility was becoming more realistic with each mile that I drove, every state that I left in my rear-view mirror, every minute that passed. Clearly, death was a possibility, but I did not focus on that thought at all, only on my duty to my family, my country, and my Corps.

I had on occasion heard my father and his friends speak about combat but that movie…that movie made the impact of those stories seem all that more real, and I knew that eventually given my choice of being an infantry officer I would be faced with similar situations. The ride was cathartic to me in that sense, and when I saw the gates of Quantico, I was mentally prepared for the next step.

CHAPTER 2
A Bit of Family History

There is no question that there are a few things in my life that were just a part of who I am. My Irish heritage for one was unavoidable and is a great source of pride for me and my entire family. My family heritage is Irish on both sides and from the time I was a child my parents taught me to be a proud Irish lad. But it wasn't always something my family spoke about, not because we weren't proud of who we were but because there was a time when being Irish in America was not really a good thing to be. So, a name that was once O'Neil changed to Neil. Now that Irish is not the stigma it used to be, we can again celebrate St. Patrick's Day the way it should be celebrated. With an abundance of family, friends, beer, and of course good old Irish whiskey.

Being Irish was not the only thing our family had to be proud about. I also came from a long line of warriors. My Great Grandfather died in the civil war fighting for an Illinois regiment that was part of the Union army. My Father was a Marine and retired a Sergeant Major. Although during WWII he was promoted to the rank of Captain in a wartime decision as did many other high ranking enlisted men at the time. After the war he reassumed the rank of

24

Sergeant Major. But would eventually retire after 30 years at the rank of Captain.

So, you can argue that it was ingrained in my DNA or that the environment I was raised in gave me a heightened sense of American pride that led to me becoming a Marine. I tend to think that it is every American's duty to do what they can to make our country the best it can be and my way of making that happen was through my service in the Marine Corps.

My parents were amazing people in their own right. My father was not just a stalwart Marine but an outstanding athlete who not only played football for the Marine Corps but played as a pro for the 1932 Chicago Bears. He toured the U.S with an all-star team, helping the Bears to help popularize pro football. My mother was an actress in silent films before she met my father and settled down and actually dated "The Duke" John Wayne himself for a while. It was kind of neat growing up with a dad who your mom obviously thought was cooler than John Wayne. They were truly in love but like all married couples they had issues from time to time.

    I can remember when my father came home from WWII. They had been married just shortly before my father shipped out for the war and hadn't had much time together. When my father arrived home, I was walking up the outside stairs and I heard a guy yelling out my mother's name. She was hanging clothes on the line, and she yelled his name back. He was in uniform but quickly dropped his seabag to hug her. She was elated that he had returned home in one piece. But I had no idea who he really was at that moment. He winked at me with a big smile on his face, walked right by me carrying my mother in his arms, tussling my hair as he passed. He took her inside and as the door closed behind them, he simply said "I'll be right back". War makes you miss the love of a good woman, and he wasn't' waiting a second longer to reunite with his wife.

After Dad returned from WWII, we bounced around quite a bit as most military families do. We moved from Barstow, San Francisco, and San Diego in California to Hawaii where he was stationed at Pearl Harbor and was the base Athletic Programmer before finally ending up back at MCRD San Diego where he would retire from the Marine Corps. He was hired at San Diego State where he would take a position as Business Manager of Athletics and eventually become the "acting" Athletic Director.

While my mother had a good career as an actress all she really wanted to do was have a family and raise her children in a good Irish tradition. Her side of the family was Irish as well, Sullivan was her family name. I never had the opportunity to meet the relatives from my mother's side of the family, but I took pride in knowing that they were from west Cork in a town called Castletownbeare, on Bantry Bay.

I had two sisters growing up. One became a schoolteacher and had two girls and a boy. The other a homemaker with three boys and a girl.

Now that you know the basics of where I came from, I can tell you about the lovely chaos of my life that was my time in the Marine Corps and a bit of how it shaped my life to come.

CHAPTER 3
OCS
The Bug and the Turtle

To Err is human; to forgive is divine.

~Alexander Pope~

Neither is Marine Corps policy.

~USMC Command ~

After the seemingly endless drive across the country, I arrived at the main gate of Marine Corps Base, Quantico, Virginia where I was greeted by the squared away sentry on duty. "Your orders to report to Officer Candidate School appear to be in order." He stated. Another sentry looking on from the guard shack, hand on his weapon and ready for anything. Growing up on Marine Corps bases around the world I had seen this, many times over, but somehow this time was different. This time I was the Marine, or at least hoped to be.

As I evaluated the situation and its difference from the many times before the sentry continued his one-sided conversation. "We have another candidate who needs to report as well but needs a ride to the school. Can you give him a ride?" "Of course," I replied reluctantly, "send him out." Little did I know what impact that ride would have on my life to come. Out of the guard, shack sauntered a powerfully built, brick of a man, standing five feet eight inches tall. John Mars was a formidable man and would not only share the ride with me to the Officer

Candidate School but would also become my bunkmate as our training moved forward.

After a few wrong turns, we reached Camp Usher, which would be our home for the weeks of training to come. We were rudely welcomed by the Sergeant of the Guard on duty, and quickly shown to the bunks that we would occupy for our time at Officer Candidate School.

I took the top bunk and Mars the lower. We settled in as much as we could, got the lay of the land. Thus, together with my new friend John Mars we began our sojourn at the officers' boot camp, euphemistically known as Officers Candidate School.

The next morning, at what seemed to be an ungodly hour, it sounded as if the hounds of hell were unleashed upon us. We were awakened by a Drill Instructor rattling a trash can with a stick, making an ungodly sound as he screamed and yelled for us to get online and stand at attention. We were a motley group and ill-prepared for the rude awakening. As I looked around in the darkness, which was somewhat illuminated by a light emanating from the quarterdeck our Drill Instructor had used for his dramatic entry into our lives, I saw an unorganized array of civilians with long hair in various states of dress and consciousness. The Drill Instructor (Marines call them Drill Instructors or DI's not Drill Sergeants), who Sergeant Bolinski, harangued and derided us through our new version of the morning routine.

We quickly discovered that the "head" (Marine for toilet) was located in an entirely separate Quonset hut some distance from our own squad bay. We were given five minutes to shit, shower and shave and get back to our barracks to form what DI Bolinski called a "walking mob." It took a good deal longer than five minutes and every second was filled with not-so-subtle motivations from DI Bolinski to move faster. Somehow, he got us all together into his walking mob and got us all the way from our barracks to the mess hall for morning chow. The day that followed could only be described as frenetic. We marched in our walking mob to and fro getting our heads shaved, drawing our clothing issue and field gear, and we marched, and marched…and marched

33

incessantly in different directions in an early effort to turn our mob into a unit.

I must admit, I thought I was going to be ahead of the game since I knew a little bit about what to expect. Having grown up in my house and with my father being a Marine Corps Sergeant Major and a former Drill Instructor I'd lived on Marine Corps bases around the world including Marine Corps Recruit Depot, San Diego. So, to a certain degree, I knew what to expect but it was all still very overwhelming. "What had I gotten myself into?"

The training area for OCS was a heavily wooded landscape, with steep, often muddy hillsides, thick swampy areas that would suck the boots right off your feet, creeks that turned into raging rivers after the slightest rainfall and being in northern Virginia the winter months were snowy and extremely cold.

The first part about any Marine Corps training is putting the trainees on the same level. They pretty much tear you down to your base and build you back up into a Marine. OCS is no different in that respect than enlisted boot camp where every enlisted Marine becomes a grunt at heart. We would later learn the value of this with our enlisted Marines. Each day in the early going was filled with marching across the parade deck and down the poorly paved roads of Camp Usher. We learned the manual of arms, how to move the rifle around our body, not our body around the rifle. The Drill Instructors made that point very clear.

We went on long runs with packs filled with everything you would typically take to the field, which in total could weigh the better part of 80 pounds.

We ran a very daunting obstacle course, did frequent physical fitness tests (PFT) and did I mention we marched in formation a lot. They did an excellent job of pushing us beyond our perceived limits and showing us what we were really made of as men. In many cases, they showed the officer candidates that they simply did not belong in the Marine Corps. Sometimes this was due to the physicality of the training, but, more often than not, it was just the mental side that caused candidates to fail. Given that this was just the beginning of our training, and we still had the six-month-long basic school to go, I must admit I was glad to see the weaker candidates leave.

Sometimes, a candidate would simply disappear with no explanation at all. They would just simply not be in our morning formation.

I was quickly appointed squad leader. A position which I remained at for the entirety of OCS. One day during one of our runs, I was dragging along another candidate that couldn't keep up the pace. A Captain who oversaw another platoon in our company, came running up to me and shouted, "Do you want him to be a 2nd Lieutenant next to you in Vietnam if he can't keep up with us on this run?". The Lieutenant's question really hit home for me. I realized that at this point in our Marine Corps training we were all being individually tested. I let the candidate drop out of my arms, and he was subsequently dropped from the training.

On a separate occasion, we had a candidate who was extremely weak physically, at least for a Marine. Thinking he could beat the system; he stuffed his pack full of newspaper on one of our "humps" (what Marine's call hiking) to lighten his load. Unbeknownst to him, the Drill Instructors would be inspecting our packs before we moved out. Our DI's were high speed, and there weren't many tricks they hadn't seen. When his ruse was discovered, they inserted a fire hose into his pack which had to weigh at least 80 pounds on its own. His lack of honor and mental fortitude had cost him and needless to say, he couldn't finish the hump, and wasn't in formation the next day.

One of our harder courses was dubbed the "Hill Trail" and was a real mother of a run. It was basically a broken leg waiting to happen. Uphill almost the entire way, narrow in width with a hill on one side and a shallow ravine on the other, with natural traps throughout for the mentally unaware like giant holes in the path and roots from trees like hands waiting to grab the boots of the unwary. We would always run Hill Trail in full gear.

If it was raining it didn't make a damn bit of difference, we still ran in the mud, sleet, snow and freezing cold. We ran Hill Trail a lot! It was not uncommon to be stepping over other candidates or literally stepping on them as we hustled to try and complete the course in the time given. Four weeks after we arrived at Camp Upshur, we were transferred out of our hole in the woods to what was known as the "Main Side" as it was the main area of the base. Marines pretty much tend to call things what they are, we don't get too fancy with the nicknames. We were assigned a barracks and squad bay which was a relic from World War II but still a vast improvement over the Quonset huts we had been staying at Camp Upshur. Hell, the head was even in the same building, and we had hot water most of the time.

Settling into our new barracks was stressful, and as Marines tend to do, we joked around a lot to help relieve that stress. The first night in that new barracks was no exception. It seems we were very close in proximity to the local train tracks and when the early morning train rumbled through it sounded like it was rolling straight through our barracks. Then out of nowhere, a voice in the dark belted out "Open the door!" Naturally the entire platoon busted out in laughter, and I nearly fell out of my rack, I laughed so hard. Shortly after our comic respite, we went through our usual morning chaos. Although we were still rough around the edges, five minutes of bathroom time each morning was starting to be enough to at least get the basics done. After morning chow our lives would change again.

Our first introduction to our new Senior Drill Instructor Sergeant Hockaday was on the drill field standing at attention.

He was a large black man who had recently returned from Vietnam. He was tough as nails, and there was no nonsense about him at all. He was here to make Marine officers because a proper officer could save lives in his eyes, and he would tolerate no half-assed efforts. We came to know him as "Boot Top High" because he vehemently insisted that when we double-timed ("run really fast") the soles of our feet better come off the ground at least as high as our boot tops. Which actually turned out to be quite helpful on the Hill Trail. He was a beyond harsh taskmaster, and each of us lived in constant fear of crossing his path in the wrong light.

My first memory of him literally left me shaking in my boots. Sergeant Hockaday was doing a platoon inspection. He stopped at the candidate next to me and using my peripheral vision (you never look directly at a Drill Instructor) I could see him ripping buttons off the candidates uniform because of some minor issue he had observed. If I could have turned invisible, I would have that very moment. Luckily, he found no defects in my uniform that day and passed me by on his way down the line.

To truly understand a Marine at heart you must first understand that all the core of all Marines is a rifleman. We all officers and enlisted alike go through boot camp and the similarities in OCS boot camp at Quantico and enlisted boot camp at either MCRD Paris Island or MCRD San Diego are many. However, I must comment that the main difference between enlisted boot camp and officer's boot camp was that while we the officer candidates were subject to mental and physical harassment on probably a much more severe scale that the enlisted men, unlike them we were never physically touched by the Drill Instructors.

John Mars and I continued to be bunk mates even though his snoring was seemingly fueled by the hounds of hell themselves and a topic of much discussion in the squad bay. I would try and fail most nights, to fall asleep before him so he wouldn't keep me up with his demon-like mouth noise. A tactic attempted by many in our platoon as well but eventually, we had enough of his monster impressions and decided to do the old "dunk his hand in warm water" trick in hopes for a little payback. Yet instead of him pissing in his pants he just woke up grumpy told us all to get fucked and started snoring again.

I ended up nicknaming my bunkmate, "Turtle" because of his short, stocky build and well, with a helmet on his head he looked just like a damn turtle in my mind. I would become known as "Tongue" and not for the glamorous reasons you might suppose. I had a habit of sticking my tongue when I was working out or running. Eventually everyone in a platoon of Marines gets a nickname no matter where you go.

We had two former enlisted men in our platoon. When these men become officers, they are commonly known as "Mustangs" in reference to the fact that although they could be taught new things, much like a mustang horse, they would always have a wild streak. Both were former Sergeants and were outstanding Marines before OCS and of immeasurable help to all the officer candidates when in need of assistance on anything we were doing, from drill to the M14.

Our Lieutenant was no slouch himself. He had two Purple Hearts from Vietnam and was a great guy although we didn't see a lot of him. We were mostly left in the hands of Sergeants Bolinski and Hockaday. We addressed our DI's by their rank and not "Sir" unlike an enlisted recruit does in boot camp. We also referred to ourselves as candidates and not recruits as enlisted Marines are required to do. We didn't talk much.

At that point, each day seemed to blur together, and it seemed as if the intensity would never let up. Even at night after all the running, marching and classes were done, we still had to get our gear ready for the next day. So, while most kids our age were going to the movies or out to a burger joint for a meal and a beer or were sitting in a bar, we were sitting in our barracks shining our boots and brass and making sure our M14 was clean and ready to go. Never have a dirty rifle, that's Marine lesson number one, and you especially didn't want a DI to find you with a dirty rifle, or you would surely pay the piper.

During the big blur in the middle of OCS, I had a run-in with another candidate by the name of Frank O'Brien. It was his squad's turn to serve chow, and it seems Frank was not particularly enamored with his task as a gravy boat operator. So, his sloppy ladle work led to him splashing gravy all over my ice cream. Being the one treat that we actually got during the week, I, of course, took this action as a personal affront to me and immediately told him he was an asshole and challenged him to a fight after chow was over. An offer which he gladly accepted yet never came to fruition since immediately after chow we were formed up into our now, not quite so unruly mob, and marched off to the barracks.

This would be my first encounter with Frank O'Brien but certainly not my last as he would eventually become one of the best friends I ever had. Funny how it works out that way sometimes.

Although I was pretty squared away and was doing well in boot camp my journey wasn't without hiccups here and there. You see I have big feet, and as such, I could not get them into the regulation tennis shoes that were given to us for some of our physical fitness testing. So instead, I had to wear my old black sneakers from college. The first time one of the DI's spotted me with those sneakers on he was all over me. He screamed his way around the platoon straight to me and asked me in a comical but severe way that only a DI can "What in God's name was I wearing on my feet?". I, of course, answered as loud as my voice would muster "Sneakers Sergeant." I was promptly ordered to "Start sneaking around the platoon."

Then for my edification and much to the amusement of my fellow candidates, I was ordered to say "Sneaking, sneaking" as I circled the platoon in my sneaker mode. This went on for at least a half an hour while the platoon engaged in other training activities.

Even though I was the "Sneaker" that day I was still squad leader and being squad leader did come with its upside, no matter how small. It's incredible to me honestly how given the right situation even the smallest of things can seem so big. You see, after morning chow the squad leaders got a five-minute head start coming back from the chow hall after morning chow. When you share a shitter with eleven other guys in your squad five minutes feels like an eternity of peace. But you can bet your ass (pun intended) that the second that five minutes was up there would be eleven guys in my face yelling for me to get off the pot.

Physical conditioning is a big part of being a Marine. In addition to regular exercise, physical fitness tests and running the Hill Trail there was also a confidence course. If you have never been on a Marine Corps confidence course, I must tell you they are aptly named. It takes all the confidence you have in yourself to get through one and not just the first time, every time. The one at OCS in Quantico was no exception to that rule. We had to walk over different elevated levels; logs were laid out to walk across without rails from one level to the next. This all had to be done without falling into the pit of freezing water below. There was also a five-story frame building that we had to

46

climb. However, the top floor had an edge that extended out farther than the other, and the only way up was a crazy gymnast ninja move or pure muscle. I was no gymnast so I would always have to muscle my way up. From the top looking down, you would finally realize what would happen if you fell. I can certainly say I was intimidated by the obstacle's height, but I wasn't the only one that's for sure.

Some Marine Corps training though just stands out more than others, and I bet you a dime to a dollar that every Marine you will ever meet has a funny story about swim qualification, and my experience was no different. No one Marine stood out just the day in general. You see as a Marine you have to be able to swim. If you cannot swim, you cannot become a Marine. We are an amphibious force after all.

Marine Corps swim qualifications are a little different than your average swim test. You start by jumping off a twelve-foot tower into a twenty-foot-deep pool in full combat gear. You must jump whether you can swim or not, there are no exceptions. And trust me when I tell you it is particularly hard to swim in full uniform with combat boots on. We also had to drop and retrieve our rifles from the bottom of the pool which was no easy task. The combination of shrieks from fear of drowning (not really possible as there are safety swimmers in the water with you) and awkward dog paddles made for a day to remember for sure. Some people, it seems, just can't swim.

One of the most memorable days of boot camp was what we called "The hike to end all hikes." Captain Duffy, our Company Commander, who just so happened to be a former reconnaissance Marine, was obviously out to prove something to us.

It was November 14th, and we were more than halfway through. We were finding ourselves, becoming Marines, maybe we were getting a little cocky, and Duffy could see. We set out on the Hill Trail at a pace so fast that three Drill Instructors from our company had to fall out. As squad leader, I started with 14 men under me, and by the time we got to the first rest stop, there were only five left standing with me. Honestly, I loved this stuff and the more physically challenging the run the more I ate it up. The more weight we carried, the faster the pace I just figured it was better for me and was making me a tougher Marine.   The little guys seemed to do better on the obstacle course than I did, and in all honesty, on the obstacle course, I was only slightly above average in my opinion. But put a pack on me and add as much weight as you want, and I was the guy at the front of the formation every time. Even Duffy's lesson couldn't stop our progress as Marine's. We were growing gradually beyond the expectations of our DI's and commanding officers. Our "Walking Mob" was now a platoon of squared away Marines officer candidates who could march in lockstep with flawless precision.

Each candidate had an M14 assigned to them, which we kept secured at the foot of our "rack" (the Marine word for bed). We learned the M14 so well that if you put one in our hands, we could strip it down and put it back together almost blindfolded. We were also introduced to the "Rifleman's Creed" and while we were not required to memorize it like the enlisted recruits, it held great weight with us as officer candidates, and many of us learned it knowing it would make us better officers.

Rifleman's Creed

This is my rifle. There are many like it, but this one is mine.

My rifle is my best friend. It is my life. I must master it as I must master my life.

Without me, my rifle is useless. Without my rifle, I am useless. I must fire my rifle true. I must shoot straighter than my enemy who is trying to kill me. I must shoot him before he shoots me. I will ...

My rifle and I know that what counts in war is not the rounds we fire, the noise of our burst, nor the smoke we make. We know that it is the hits that count. We will hit ...

My rifle is human, even as I, because it is my life.

Thus, I will learn it as a brother. I will learn its weaknesses, its strength, its parts, its accessories, its sights, and its barrel.

I will keep my rifle clean and ready, even as I am clean and ready.
We will become part of each other. We will ... Before God, I swear this creed.
My rifle and myself are the defenders of my country. We are the masters of our enemy. We are the saviors of my life. So be it, until there is no enemy, but peace. Amen.

The training was top notch but stressful and not without risk of bodily harm each day. In fact, at one point during our training after a particularly long run, I passed some blood. So much so that the candidate next to me literally passed out as he saw the blood fall from my body. I was taken to see a doctor and ordered to go to Bethesda Naval Hospital for further treatment. The next day I was outfitted with a semi-official Marine Corps dress uniform since we had only been issued our utilities to that point. I was then transported to Bethesda, not really knowing what to expect or even what might be wrong with me. After quite a long wait I was escorted into a treatment room. Two Navy corpsmen came in and told me to get undressed, which I promptly did. I then lay down on the examination table wholly nude, and they proceeded to strap me down and take up positions on either side of me. I was less than happy about my current situation.

The doctor, who I would later learn was a urologist, entered shortly after that and picked up a long instrument off the nearby surgical tray. I knew where it was going, and to me, it looked like it was the size of a baseball bat. Now I knew why they had strapped me down. The doctor looked me in the eye and said, "Marine, this is going to hurt a little bit." To this day that is still the biggest understatement I have ever heard.

He then proceeded to put the instrument straight up my penis through my urethra and into my kidney for examination as the two corpsmen held me down. No anesthetic. No bedside manner. No explanation. Military doctors, you got to love them.

After what seemed like an eternity of absolute agony, he withdrew the instrument, tossed it back on the surgical tray and said he saw nothing to be concerned with and I could go back to duty ASAP, and just as quickly as he had come in, he left with no further instruction.

The corpsmen that had been holding me down proceeded to unstrap me from the table, helped me to my feet and helped me get dressed. I was still bleeding profusely from my penis and was so weak from the pain I could barely stand. But they helped me find the driver who brought me, and I was expeditiously shuttled back to Quantico.

Once I was back in my platoon area, I recovered quickly. I changed out of my dress uniform into my utilities, found out from the fire watch where the platoon was and joined them. Getting sick is something no Marine ever wants to do, and that goes double while you are in OCS. You get too ill, and they cycle you back to another platoon. Extending your stay, and thus your struggle to make it through what is one of the most challenging times of every Marine's life.

However, as it was, the worst was yet to come. That night around 0200 in the morning, I started to feel as if someone was kicking me square in the balls every sixty seconds or so. It was the absolute worst pain

I have ever experienced in my life. And before you ask...yes, it was worse than what the doctor shoved up my penis. Turned out that I was passing a blood clot through my kidney from the rough examination that the urologist had given me earlier that day. I was laying on the floor of the squad bay in absolute agony. John Mars found the watch officer, and in short order, an ambulance came and took me to the base hospital at Quantico. The doctor on duty then gave me some quite effective pain medication, and I quickly passed out for the rest of the evening. In the morning I awoke pain-free, the clot had passed, and I was good to go. I once again raced back to the platoon and was allowed to continue my training without interruption.

Toward the end of every Marine's boot camp training, you are tasked with a final operation that simulates what real combat is like as strictly as possible without the live fire. Today it is called "The Crucible" in 1966 it was called a "3 Day War" and it is one of the most arduous and exhausting things you go through at any stage of your

Marine Corps career.

During our 3 Day War, we pretended to fight the enemy. We dug real foxholes and engaged in tactical war games against our simulated enemy. In this particular case enlisted Marines were pretending to be our adversaries, all of whom were Vietnam veterans and who took great delight in taunting and tormenting prospective officer candidates.

I got particularly pissed off one night by these enlisted Marines. I had set up an ambush wherein we shot them at close range and even though we were using blanks it still hurt quite a bit if you shot someone from close range. They all started screaming and yelling that we were too close to be firing at them. I told them they could go screw themselves and they should learn to take their own medicine or quit doing what they had been doing to us. We didn't get harassed by them anymore, that's for sure.

It was also cold; in fact, it was freezing. We literally froze our butts off at night and the daytime wasn't much better. On the last night of the operation, Mars and I were sharing a foxhole, and we were surrounded by our simulated enemy on all sides. I was so extremely cold just lying there in our foxhole neither one of us could stand it, and he volunteered for a secret mission to end our suffering.

It seems that Mars knew the location of the platoons sleeping bags. The DI's wouldn't let us use them and were guarding them carefully. Mars proposed crawling to their position and trying to bring one back to our foxhole. I took his rifle and kept firing both his rifle and my own while he undertook the secret mission to warm our butts. He returned quicker than I expected with a sleeping bag in tow and for the next three or four hours we managed to stay warm by getting really close together in that sleeping bag. We continued to fire our weapons from the minimal warmth of our sleeping bag lined foxhole at our mock enemy and just before first light Mars crawled back, returned the sleeping bag, and no one was ever the wiser. It has never ceased to amaze me how inventive extreme cold, or heat can make a Marine.

We had finished our 3 Day War and were marching back to our barracks in the dark of night when a battalion jeep drove up to our column. I was called over by our platoon commander and informed that I had a telegram. They showed it to me, but it was so dark I couldn't read anything. I shouted through my exhaustion "The candidate cannot read the telegram it is too dark sir." And just like that a flashlight magically appeared. I read the telegram. It was from my father who had sent it to congratulate me on passing the bar exam. At that point though, I could have cared less about anything. All I wanted after three sleep-deprived days was some hot chow, a shower, and some sleep.

Thankfully our Lieutenant being the good man he was, he marched us right out of the field and into the mess hall. I must have eaten a dozen eggs and just as many pancakes with Mars urging me to eat more. Then it was back to the squad bay were, of course, we first cleaned all our dirty gear and then hit the rack for the next 18 hours.

Refreshed from our long sleep, our next task was the physical readiness test. It was one of the more difficult tests we had to perform. It was a timed event, and your score weighed heavily on how you did in your platoon and your company and as you may have already guessed, it was highly competitive.

The event consisted of a rope climb in full gear, a step up through the multilevel log obstacle, a 40-yard dash to pick up a simulated wounded Marine then bringing him back to the start in a fireman's carry, followed by a three-mile run in full combat gear.

Since I was the second biggest candidate in our platoon at 190 pounds, I was stuck with candidate Callahan who weighed in at around 240 pounds. Now it was kind of an unwritten rule by this point that you would help your partner in this event by cooperating on the fireman's carry drill. Making it marginally more manageable for your partner to get to his feet with you on his back. Callahan, however, refused this method despite my entreaties of him to assist me since he was so heavy, and I had difficulty getting him off the ground in earlier efforts.

Since time was such a critical factor in this event though I formulated a plan. I told everyone to watch as I carried out my plan to a tee. I ran down to Callahan as fast as my feet would take me and kicked him square in the balls with all I had. He immediately leaped to his feet; I slung him over my shoulder in record time. Luckily none of the Di's cared for Callahan too much. A fact which was quite evident from the smirks on their faces that they enjoyed my act that day.

A few weeks into OCS we learned there was a Junior Officer's Professional Association down in Washington D.C. JOPA, as it was called, which had events two or three times a week and officer candidates were welcome to join in the festivities.

Since I was one of the few candidates that had a car if we got liberty (time off during the work week in Marine speak), which we did after our fourth week. Generally, Saturday night or Sunday afternoon and sometimes both. I would drive as many candidates as I could fit in the old Volkswagen bug down to D.C., which generally consisted of about six of us total and did not make for a comfortable ride at all.

We would stop at the main gate on the way out and grab a six pack for each man quickly learning that the beer math meant Washington D.C. was precisely a six pack away.

With our completely shaved heads, we weren't really popular with the local college girls but with the secretaries and other working-class types on Capitol Hill we did pretty well for ourselves. To this day I can still hear the song "Winchester Cathedral" by The New Vaudeville Band ringing in my ears. It sorts of became our marching song every time we sojourned to Washington D.C.

Sometimes during training things would happen that were just downright funny. I remember one incident just a few days before our graduation from boot camp. You see, whenever we were marching and had to cross a railroad track on the main side, we had to post guards out to give us the "all clear" to cross the track.

This particular day we were being marched by Sergeant Bolinski, although by now it was not uncommon for one of the candidates, frequently myself, to be out front giving the marching orders. Sergeant Bolinski was marching us down the road like a thousand time before and yelled: "train guards out." This notified the second man on both outside squads to double-time it to the train tracks and take up a post on the tracks at parade rest. At that point, they were each individually supposed to give the "all clear" for their perspective side, port or starboard. That day we clearly heard the call "all clear on the starboard side" and then waited on the same from the port side and waited.

Being concerned with no report from the port side guard our fearless DI yelled out "report from the port side" and still there was no report.

Simultaneously we heard an approaching train quickly followed by the woeful cry coming from the guard on the port side "it's not clear on the port!". Sergeant Bolinski halted the platoon and screamed with all he had at the dumbstruck candidate who was frozen like a deer in the headlights right on the tracks. "Get your ass off the track you dumb shit" he exclaimed, waking the candidate from his glassy-eyed stare just in time for him to beat a hasty retreat to the platoon, narrowly missing being flattened by the train. We all had a good laugh at that one later. What can I say, sometimes Marines have a slightly twisted sense of humor?

With only two days to go before our graduation, the platoon was out in front of formation for morning chow, and our platoon commander was standing out front reading off a list of candidate names. Strangely, but most likely for the best, those candidates fell out of formation that morning, and we never saw them again. They had, to their own misfortune, lasted through it all, right to the very end but had failed to meet the ultimate test the approval of our platoon sergeants and platoon commander. You cannot be a good leader of men if you do not have the faith of your commanders above as well as the troops around you and those candidates failed in a critical part of that task.

That very evening, for the first time, we were left on our own without Drill Instructors to march us to and from evening chow. As it happened, I was the acting platoon commander on that day, and it was my responsibility to march the platoon back from evening chow. As we marched back in the darkness, looking smart, all-in lockstep, we could all feel it, we were ready to become Marines. Someone started whistling the theme song from
"The Bridge Over the River Kwai" and before I knew the entire platoon was whistling along. I even joined in and even without my cadence to lead the platoon we comfortably stayed in step and looked like a high-speed platoon of squared away Marines.

As I looked over the platoon in the darkness and up onto the platform by our barracks, I saw the eyes of Sergeant Hockaday peering out from the shadows. I would swear to this day, although he would never have admitted it, I saw a grin on his face as we marched by whistling. I was the only one who saw him in the shadows that night but the night before we graduated

Sergeant Hockaday bought the platoon a keg of beer which didn't last very long in a squad bay filled with young Marine officer candidates. We learned that night that Sergeant Hockaday was a really nice guy and I thank him to this day for the wisdom and training he bestowed upon my fellow candidates and me as there is little doubt as several points during my career it saved my life.

The next day was our graduation, and we had a ceremony over on the main side. My second lieutenant bars (referred to as butter bars by Marines) were pinned on by some Private First Class like everyone else's were. We then had to give the PFC two dollars as a sign of respect to our new rank and got our first salute from them as an officer.

Although I was eager to go celebrate with the rest of my newly commissioned officers, I had permission to leave early for a wedding I had to attend in San Diego, so I hopped in my Volkswagen bug and raced to the airport. I must admit I was feeling pretty good and proud to be headed home to San Diego, a brand spanking new 2nd Lieutenant in full uniform.

The rest of my fellow candidates were free to go the next day and most headed back to their hometowns for a little R & R.

Next on our agenda was "The Basic School."

CHAPTER 4
The Basic School(part 1)
A Finishing School

All Marines, officer and enlisted alike, receive the best training of any military service in the world. We all go through boot camp and after we all go through a secondary training school which differs depending on your choice of a career track.

For officer's, if OCS was the version of boot camp, then "The Basic School" (TBS) was our finishing school. Aside from the OCS graduates that went directly to flight school, we all reported to The Basic School a few days before Christmas. Luckily, we were then promptly released to go home and spend the holidays with our prospective families.

I was released a day earlier than the rest of my class at my special request to attend a wedding in San Diego, and I reported back on New Year's Eve Day. Of course, I was promptly assigned as the Officer of the Day upon my return and spent New Year's Eve

1966 on duty missing a fantastic opportunity to ring in the new year at a party in D.C.

The difference between OCS and TBS was dramatic. We were officers now, so we got a bit of an upgrade over our previous living conditions. We had two-man rooms and shared a head with the room next door. Compared to OCS it was like staying at the Ritz.

Several of us were assigned as "sponsors" or "host Marines" to Marines from other allied armed services around the world. I was appointed as the sponsor for a Korean Captain by the name of Yung "YC" Kong. His actual name was Yung Chul. YC and I had some issues at first due to his poor English and my complete lack of Korean.

John "Turtle" Mars also wound up in my platoon and on my floor just a couple of doors down from me. He was assigned as the sponsor for a Thai Marine by the name of Chuddabudi. There was also a Peruvian Marine and a Vietnamese Marine in our platoon. These Marines were sent by their respective countries to go through our training and take that knowledge back to their units in their homeland. This is a pretty common practice, and we carry it out to this day throughout the world.

Luckily there were some familiar faces in our platoon from OCS. As I mentioned John Mars was there but so were Frank O'Brien, John Norris, Warren Pinckert, and Wayne Manson. Each of us had a sponsor Marine assigned to us and shared a room with them as well. We had bunk beds in our rooms, so I took the top and YC took the bottom.

The chow hall at TBS was fantastic. We could select the food we wanted to eat here, which was in high supply. We never lacked for calories that's for sure, and we burned them up as quickly as we consumed them. The best part though was no DI screaming at you. We actually had a reasonable amount of time to eat. Although we still ate quickly out of habit.

There was even a bar at TBS which was open every night called "The Flying Bridge." It was a popular place to grab a beer and relax when we actually got some time off.

Much of our time was spent in the field where we were taught lifesaving tactical skills like how to set up an ambush, the proper way to patrol and the like. The rest of our time was spent in the classroom learning how exactly to be an officer in classes like tactics, logistics, regulations, etc.

One of our most important yet most difficult and time-consuming courses was map reading and the use of a compass and protractor. We learned how to identify and resect from a known object such as a mountain and other land features. To find out our exact position using a protractor, ruler, and a compass in conjunction with the map. This course was initially taught in the classroom but of course, had to be perfected in real time in the field. There were many days where we relied on only our map and compass to find objectives. It was a course that every 2nd Lieutenant must pass and could only do so by finding specific locations which were actual markers with numbers on them spread throughout the woods of Quantico. You see the number; you report back if you found the right number you were good to go.

My problem on the day we were tested was remembering that there was a "magnetic declination" that had to be considered to find the right locations. In other words, a certain number of degrees had to be subtracted from the protractor to account for the number of degrees the compasses changed because of the position of Quantico as it related to the magnetic pole. Welcome to the beautiful world of compass reading. This, in all honesty, is still a bit of a mystery to me to this day, but the course had to be done, and on that day, I failed to do it properly. I had to retake the course and was quite upset with myself as it was really the first time, I had failed at any task that had been put before me since I joined the Marine Corps.

The day I had to retake the course I initially forgot about the magnetic declination again, thanks to some heavy drinking the night before I'm sure, and I had to rush back and do the entire course again before it got dark.

I finally completed the course during a torrential downpour and had to forge two creeks that had turned into raging rivers. During one river crossing, I got tangled up in a fallen tree crossing the river which I feared I would never be able to extricate myself from. But my determination to not drown and to pass the course ruled out, and I won the day. I can tell you though that I was not alone on that day, and I am pretty sure the hills of Quantico are filled to this day with 2nd Lieutenants with a map and a compass trying to find the right number. Even though we can find locations using GPS technology now the

Marine Corps still teaches the old method as well for good measure.

On January 26th, 1967, I received a notification that I was going to be sworn into the bar by Justice Homer Ferguson of the Court of Military Appeals. A luncheon was hosted by General Masters, the Commanding General of the Marine Corps Schools and Colonel Castle, the Commanding Officer of The Basic School. It was a big deal, and I was quite honored that my commanding officers went to the trouble to celebrate my achievement in such a way. However, where I really wanted to be in the field with my company, and I managed to ditch the luncheon early and get back to my unit as soon as possible.

Our arms training at TBS went beyond just our M14. We got to train with rifle grenades and the old fashioned 3.5 bazooka, a remnant of the Korean War. But the primary weapon we utilized was still our M14, the predecessor to the M16, it was a reliable weapon which was incredibly accurate and extremely durable under adverse conditions, even when not cleaned regularly.

We had one day during TBS that we got to work with the M16. I was not impressed with the rifle at all, but we would not be fully introduced to the M16 and what a piece of crap it really was until we reached Vietnam.

In addition to the M14, our other base weapon was the Colt 1911 .45 pistol. We practiced with it frequently and learned to strip it down and put it back together by feel just as we had the M14. This skill would prove invaluable to me during my time in Vietnam.

In February of 1967, we again had the opportunity to fire the 3.5 bazookas and this time we even got to use the M2A1-7 flamethrower. It had a handheld section where the flame came out and you didn't want to make a mistake, or it could cost you a hand. It was a supremely effective weapon for its purpose, but wow was it a heavy mother, and of course, I was the one to tow it for our platoon as we made a simulated attack on a static position. That thing really threw some heat I can tell you.

We continued our patrolling and ambush exercises and learned how to utilize a compass at night as well. Educating ourselves on how to walk off distances when it was too dark to read a map and too dangerous to break out a flashlight. This would become an essential skill when trying to set up ambushes and patrols in Vietnam, giving us the skills to place our teams in the right position and ensuring you weren't putting your men in more risk of harm than absolutely necessary.

One of my biggest problems during TBS developed not long after we got there. There was usually snow on the ground, and when there wasn't snow, there was either sleet or rain that seemed so cold it made you wish for snow.

Because of my more significant than average size 13 feet and the fact that the only pair of size 13 boots on the base belonged to a Marine in a company two months ahead of my own. I was forced to go through the first four months of TBS without thermal boots and regular boots instead. I was literally freezing my feet off. Northern Virginia can be brutal during the winter months, and all I could think was...Isn't Vietnam supposed to be hot? Cold is bad, cold, and wet is worse but cold wet feet is something that can stop you in your tracks. Not sure if it was the thoughts of warmer weather, layers of socks or just dumb luck but I made it through TBS with all my toes intact.

TBS was located in an extremely isolated section of Quantico. Deep into the Northern Virginia woods. We had to drive for what seemed like hours after leaving the main highway to reach our barracks at TBS. I was lucky to have my VW bug and took every opportunity I got to head down to Washington D.C. and hit up the Irish bars trying to meet girls. Matt Kane's was the go-to bar at the time and my car was always loaded down with a minimum six 2nd Lieutenants if I made the trip to D.C. and we consistently applied the six pack away rule on the ride down.

My Dad, retired from the Marine Corps, was now working for Equitable Life Insurance. He was coming to Washington D.C. on business, so I asked him to bring my old record player to me, along with some of my records. I had an eclectic taste in music, and he brought out a bunch of my collection. I was in music heaven. I set up the record player in my room and soon began entertaining YC and myself as well as the other members of our platoon who would often gather in our room. We could bring beer into our rooms at TBS, and after a long day in the field, all we really wanted to do was crash out, sip a cold one and listen to some good music. It really helped us relax and take the edge off some very long and stressful days at TBS.

In March of 1967, we went to the rifle range to qualify with not only our M14 rifles but the Colt 1911 .45 pistol as well. As luck would have it though, on the day we went to qualify after weeks of practice the weather had its own ideas for the day. It was 18 degrees with a 25 mile an hour wind whipping across the range. Trying to shoot my rifle under those conditions was one of the most challenging things I've ever had to do.

You had to take your gloves off to shoot the M14, and the freezing cold made it difficult to even feel the trigger. The Vietnamese Marine attached to our platoon literally stood up on the rifle range, threw his rifle down, saying "Fuck this shit" and refused to shoot. He then marched back to the cattle truck that brought us to the range that day and sat down. There was nothing anyone could do to discipline him since technically he wasn't part of our unit, lucky bastard.

I managed to barely qualify with the rifle that day, but I did qualify as a high expert with the pistol. It was surely an experience I will always remember and without question one of the most miserable days of my life. Many of the Marines and Lieutenants that shot with me on that day did not qualify and were forced to retake the entire course.

As I stated earlier, we spent most of our time in the field, since that was where we would most likely all end up anyway. And in the spring of 1967, I led my first patrol at TBS. A Marine Captain by the name of Paddy Collins was our instructor on that day. He was a Marine Corps icon, extremely tough and incredibly demanding and even made us repeat a river crossing once because we did not cross it in the manner in which he had directed us to do so. I'm talking about water so cold that it makes all your manhood shrivel up and try to hide. Later we would become friends, but he treated me no differently than the rest of the Marines even though I was older and more experienced in some ways.

We did a few days of helicopter training during that spring as well. Vietnam would become the war of the helicopter, and I would spend plenty of time on them and with them during the war. We practiced coming into a landing zone that was contested (hot LZ's). Blanks were fired at us as we landed in the helicopters, and it was quite surreal to run off the aircraft and hear rounds going off all around you.

It was excellent training with enlisted Marines playing the part of the VC. Sometimes the aggressors would be quite spirited, and with Marines being Marines, more than once there was the threat of actual violence breaking out.

Once while observing another platoon fighting their simulated VC enemy, I saw that they had run out of blank rounds. The acting Platoon Commander then ordered the 2nd Lieutenants to fix bayonets, and they charged into their aggressors. The enlisted Marines quickly turned tail and ran. Or as we say in the Marine Corps, they attacked in the opposite direction.

CHAPTER 5
The Basic School (part 2)
Every Marine is an O3

We were informed at some point during TBS that we would actually be going on a live amphibious operation and tactical landing at Virginia Beach. To prepare for this task, we had a high wall from which we climbed and descended on netting, much like the netting that we would use on board the amphibious ship when the time came. While it was tough going in full combat gear making your way down the rope netting, it was nothing like the reality to come.

When the schedule came up for us to get on board the ship for the exercise, we were all highly anticipating the break away from Quantico and joked about how we would enjoy our sojourn down to Virginia Beach. What a surprise we had in store for us.

We were bussed down to Virginia Beach and boarded the amphibious transport ship operated by "the world's greatest taxi service" the United States Navy. We were then schooled in the protocol on how to board a Navy ship. First requesting permission to come aboard, saluting the flag and OOD and wait for permission to board to be given. What we were not schooled on however was what to expect once we were below decks.

Our quarters consisted of three high rack bunk beds crammed in head to toe, bunk to bunk. It was pretty much a sardine can for Marines. The seas were somewhat rough, and although there was scuttlebutt (Marine for gossip) about the operation being canceled, we pulled out of port anyway. Not long after we began our journey on the open ocean many of the 2nd Lieutenants started throwing up. Quickly the sinks and toilets were filled to the brim and clogged with vomit. It was not a pretty sight and the smell. Let's just say it was not my favorite perfume.

For some reason, I still can't explain why I took the middle bunk. The Lieutenant above me kept heaving his lunch from on high, and

I would have to hold my hand out before I came out of my rack. Then, of course, I had the pleasure of stepping in his vomit when I hit the deck.

We were ordered to sleep in our utilities, with our rifles in our rack and all our combat gear next to us, ready to go at a moment's notice. That first night on the ocean was a blur of vomiting and pounding seas.

The next morning, we were rousted from our racks by the blaring sounds of "Man your battle stations and prepare to disembark" blaring over the PA system. We were then sent to our pre-arranged stations after we were hauled up on deck.

Since I was one of the bigger guys in our platoon, myself and two other Marines of comparable size lead the way over the side to the bouncing Mike boat (WWII landing craft) below. We were then instructed to hold the netting outboard from the ship to ease the way for our fellow Marines as they followed down the netting. With no one to hold the netting for us, however, it was pretty rough going carrying a full combat pack plus, rifle, helmet, etc. but luckily the three of us made it safely down the netting to the well of the Mike boat.

We then held the netting for our fellow officers, and everyone made it safely into the boat. Once onboard we began to circle since in good old Marine Corps "hurry up and wait" fashion we were not going to land on the beach until all the landing craft were filled, and we could hit the beach in successive waves, not one at a time. I was the acting platoon commander at the time, and the seas were still somewhat rough. Marines began to promptly throw up again inside the Mike boat being unable to reach the sides. We were packed in asshole to elbow, and at one point I noticed a young South American 2nd Lieutenant was about to lose his lunch, I told him to make for the side of the boat. He confidently said to me over and over "I'm not going to throw up" just before losing it all over me. We were all wearing web gear that held our canteens, extra gear and the like, and his vomit was enmeshed in every piece of equipment I had on from the neck down.

Finally, after what seemed like forever and to the melodious laughter of the sailors on board who were used to the motion of the waves, we began our approach to the shore.

We had been warned not to fix our bayonets but to simply charge off the boat and form up to get right back on the Mike boats to be brought back to the amphibious ship we came out on. To me, that wasn't Marine training, that was dog and pony crap. I said to hell with it and ordered everyone to fix bayonets. We weren't going to let anybody stand in our way when we hit the beach.

When that ramp came down, we charged off the boat screaming like wild Indians on the attack, with bayonets out for all to see, much to the surprise and delight of the reporters and onlookers standing on the beach. Once on shore, I called a halt to our dramatic charge, and we patiently waited until we were told to reboard the Mike boat and head back to our amphibious ship.

The return to our amphibious ship was much more complicated. By the time we had loaded up and trudged out to the ship the bottom of the Mike boat was filled with an aromatic soup of seawater, vomit, and diesel fuel, so we were already feeling less than our best. We pulled alongside the ship, and they dropped in the nets. The two other Marines that helped me secure the nets when we were loading out again helped me secure the nets for the rest of our stick. As the waves took the Mike boat up and down the diesel fuel and vomit mixture were now dropping down all over us making more men sick and just adding to the fun.

When it came time for us to climb the netting, they were slippery with vomit and fuel and quite treacherous. It took all the strength and focus that I had to climb that netting and fell just short of a miracle that all three of us made it to the back onto the mother ship without injury. In fact, on one of the adjacent Mike boats, one of the Lieutenants lost his grip, fell in between the Mike boat and the mother ship, and ended up breaking his leg. Frankly, he was fortunate he had not lost his life.

That night we attempted to find the sailors who were laughing at us while we struggled on board the Mike boats. More than one brawl took place that night. The very next day the seas were incredibly calm. We made a second amphibious landing, and wouldn't you know it, everything went off without a hitch.

Nowadays when you join the Marine Corps, you go through a careful process of selecting your Military Occupational Specialty (MOS) but back then in TBS you only put in for your MOS when you passed a certain point in your training. Not really any better or worse than how it is done now; it's just the way things were done back then. When it came my time, of course, I put in for 03 (Infantry).

I was called in shortly after by my Platoon Commander, Captain Chapin. He questioned me about my choice and the fact that the Marine Corps needed lawyers. I explained to him that I had joined the Marine Corps with the promise from my recruiter that I could be a 03 officer and that I felt the Marine Corps owed me that opportunity and that I was not going to change my request. He then gave me a direct order to put down lawyer as my first choice. I said, "Go to Hell, I am not changing it." The very next day I was called to the Company Commander's office. I reported to Major Broad and smartly snapped to attention as I did. He sternly said to me "I understand that you refused a direct order from your Platoon Commander to designate JAG as your primary MOS request." To which I replied: "Yes Sir." Major Broad then leaned back with a face of stone and continued his questioning "I also understand you told Captain Chapin to go to hell when he gave you that order." My reply again was "Yes Sir." Major Broad said to me "If I was to give you the same order would your answer be the same to me?" my retort was "yes sir". A smile crept across Major Broad's face as he told me to get out of his office. I immediately about-faced and double-timed out of his office laughing under my breath because I knew my request to be a 03 officer was going to be granted.

The most essential truth about the life of a Marine is that it really boils down to one thing if you're a Marine you are a 03. You may learn other disciplines and skills, but every Marine is a grunt at heart. That is how Marines have been trained from the start, and that is how we train Marines to this very day.

One weekend during March at TBS we got a weekend pass, and my classmate Wayne Manson suggested we go visit a friend of his in Baltimore, Maryland. His friend was a fellow Marine, a recipient of the Navy Cross and had been with Chesty Puller at the Chosin Reservoir. Marines refer to them as The Frozen Chosen, and few Marines are held in higher regard. So, John Mars, Wayne Manson, 2nd Lieutenant LuLi and I jumped into a car and went up to Baltimore to meet Wayne's friend.

We had a great weekend except for a small problem that developed the first night after a long night of drinking in downtown Baltimore. We had gotten into a pretty big brawl that night in an after-hours breakfast place. As I said we had been drinking heavily and I had to hit the head, as I was exiting the head, there was a large group of long-haired types crowding the hallway. In proper Marine Corps style, I shouted, "Make a hole," and of course one of the long hairs turned to me and said in his smart tone "Did you call me an asshole?" With that, I punched him square in the nose, and the brawl began. We did a pretty good job of kicking their butts, and in short order, all the long hairs exited the restaurant under duress.

The next evening, however, we made the mistake of going back to the same after-hours breakfast place for something to eat after another night of drinking. When we exited the restaurant, we found a rock had penetrated our car's windshield leaving a large hole on the driver's side. Unfortunate as that was, it was only the beginning of our problem. We had to drive back to Quantico the next day in the freezing cold weather. Strangely enough, Baltimore is also precisely a six-pack away from Quantico, beer math, go figure.

We were all taught to field strip the M60 machine gun and learned how to effectively use 60mm and 81mm mortars. In fact, about the only test that I really ever studied hard for in TBS was on the 81mm mortars as it was my understanding that they would most likely be the primary supporting weapon that we could rely upon in the field. 81mm mortars are quite sufficient for a rifle company. Yes, we could carry the M60 with us, but nothing was quite as effective in a firefight as the support from an 81mm mortar. We also did some work with the M79 grenade launcher. This was a shotgun style breakaway gun that fired one 40mm grenade and was very effective against the enemy at close range. In other words, if you mastered it properly, you could elevate the gun and fire a round so that the grenade would drop right in on the enemy's head.

The brass tacks of it all though is, even with all the excellent training we had at TBS it was the intimate knowledge of our instructors that gave it value. Their instruction on ambushing and patrolling would turn out to be absolutely crucial to our survival once we reached Vietnam. I am to this day deeply indebted to those instructors for what they taught us. Basically, they taught us how to survive in what would be our own version of hell on earth.

We also did a lot of work on our hand-to-hand combat skills. My good friend, Frank

O'Brien, was my counterpart in-hand-to-hand because we were about the same size. However, our hand-to-hand classes were not always friendly scuffles.

We were taught in our hand-to-hand classes how to choke out an enemy to make him lose consciousness by cutting off the blood flow to the brain from the carotid artery, thus depriving the brain of oxygen. One day, Frank must have been carrying a grudge from the night before or something, and he decided just to choke me instead of cutting off the blood flow from the carotid artery. I was literally choking to death. I was trying to tell him to choke me out or let me go but couldn't speak. After he had a good laugh, he let me go.

An hour or so after the choke we were working with the bayonet and hand to hand combat. He was barehanded, and I had the bayonet on my rifle attacking him. I intentionally gave him a small cut on the hand, and as he winced in pain he said, "Why did you do that?". My reply, "Fuck you, O'Brien. Don't ever choke me out like you did before." We had a good laugh about the day after he bandaged up his hand and were best friends from that day on. In fact, he and I used to frequent a bar in Washington D.C. called Matt Kane's famous for taking care of Marines that unfortunately no longer exists.

We were taught at TBS how to properly wear our uniforms and the Marine Corps history behind them as well. To complete our schooling, we had to have tailored uniforms that we had to pay for, although we were given an initial uniform allowance that did not cover the cost of dress blues, dress whites, summer khakis or winter greens. We also had to buy a sword for ceremonial purposes and had hours of training on how to use it properly for parade purposes. We all joked of course of how we would use our swords in the jungles of Vietnam.

It was on liberty all the way through OCS and TBS; in fact, where we as Marines were reminded of the dissension that existed in America against the Vietnam War. It was difficult for us to pick up or even talk to some women on liberty because our hair was too short and a dead giveaway to the anti-war types. Other women were friendlier, and while anti-war sentiment was quite widespread, we were treated well before going to Vietnam. Coming back would prove to be something much different and an entirely new form of a battle for those of us lucky enough to return.

Not only did we learn massive amounts of life-saving information while at OCS and TBS, but we formed friendships and bonds that would never be broken. Wayne Manson gained the nickname "Bands of Steel" because when he was asked to stand up and talk about the M60 machine gun, he spouted off about "bands of steel" coming from the M60, and it got quite a laugh from all of us. It was straight out of the manual for the M60, and he was on point it was just one of those moments.

John Norris, one of the few married members of our platoon, was married to a woman by the name of Connie. We all liked John quite a bit and joked with Connie that if John was ever killed, we were all going to come back and marry her. Little did we know.

Frank O'Brien and I, of course, became best friends and I remain incredibly close with Turtle and by the time of graduation was close to YC as well. In fact, the day that we were graduating as I looked down at YC shining his boots, I knew he had fully grasped the English language (or at least the Marine Corps version of it) as he looked up at me with a smile and proclaimed "Another fucking day in the Corps." I knew that very moment YC was one of us.

I was pretty lucky come our graduation day to have sold my car to another 2nd Lieutenant in one of the other classes behind us. As soon as the graduation ceremony was over, I said my goodbyes and beat feet to the airport for the flight home. We all got 30 days of leave before we were to report for duty at Norton Air Force Base in California to catch our flight to Okinawa and then from there to Vietnam. Frank elected to come to San Diego with me for leave rather than go home to Wheeling, West Virginia. The next 30 days would become some of the best days of my life.

MAY   67

96

CHAPTER 6
30 Days of leave
A pre-war party

Have I mentioned how much I love California yet? Trick question, I know I have I just wanted to make it abundantly clear that it is my favorite place in the world. Although it is getting a bit crowded these days.

After we graduated from TBS Frank O'Brien and I headed back to California for our 30 days of pre-war leave. In those days we always flew in uniform as we were able to fly with a tremendous discount or free of charge depending upon the seat availability on a civilian aircraft.

On the flight home, I reflected much on the last nine months. The seriousness of the training, the cold of the Quantico winter, and the irony that we would soon be heading to one of the more hot and humid climates on the planet. But for the majority of the long

97

flight, I reflected on my own mortality and if I would make it through my 13-month tour in Vietnam.

Little did I know as I flew over America staring out the window at the vast beauty of our nation that all of us who had opted to be 03's, 13 of us from our platoon alone at TBS, would face such a high casualty rate. In fact, the frequency of an amputation or crippling injury in Vietnam would be 300 times higher than it was in WWII.

The first thing I did when I got back to San Diego was to spend some time with my parents. I could tell that they were both delighted to see me and were proud of me for my decision to serve my country as a United States Marine, especially my father. But there was also a cloud of darkness in them as they knew that I would soon be leaving for Vietnam.

I linked up with my good friends Jon Low, Ray Ratelle and Scott from San Diego State University and spent part of my time on leave living with them in La Jolla. The rest of the time I spent with my folks. Frank O'Brien basically crashed at my parents' house the entire time and was a welcome addition to the family. YC even came out and spent a few days with all of us.

Jon and Scott were both working as stockbrokers and doing quite well for themselves as bachelors in La Jolla. Jon introduced me to a hairdresser by the name of Kathy, and we hit it off really well. She loved to have a good time, and that was what I needed at the time. All I really cared about in those days was getting laid and drinking as much cold beer as I could get my hands on.

Frank and I spent a lot of time in Mission Beach and quickly proclaimed "The Beachcomber" our favorite bar. There was a plethora of college girls in Mission Beach as well as secretaries, Marine and Navy officers.

Frank and I ran every day and ate as much as we could trying to pack on some weight, knowing we would be losing the pounds we packed on in the months to come. We also drank like there was no tomorrow, because honestly soon there might not be in our eyes. I would estimate we spent 90 percent of our waking hours at the Beachcomber Bar in Mission Beach, trying to either pick up girls or just downing cold brews.

I had gone to Guadalajara Mexico in the summer between my second and third year of law school and absolutely fell in love with Puerta Vallarta. In fact, I had even met the future Mayor of Puerto Vallarta, Luis Favela, and he and I became good friends. So, I talked Frank into going down to Puerto Vallarta for some fun, and we asked Kathy along with us. Frank went down a few days before Kathy and me, and when we arrived at the hotel, which consisted of just some bungalows on the beach. Frank was laying on a hammock, laughing at us as we approached. What ensued was a beer-filled blur and one hell of a great ten days.

Before I left, I knew I wanted to reach out to as many people as I could since I might never see them again, a thought that was constantly in the back of my mind. So, I went around to all my high school and college friends as well as my neighbors and spent a reasonable amount of time catching up.

One of our neighbors was Red Callahan and his family. Red and my father had been in the Marine Corps together for 30 years and even bought houses out by San Diego State together. Their oldest son, John Callahan, was enlisting in the Army intending to go to Vietnam as a paratrooper. I had known Johnny since he was a little boy and he and I basically grew up together even though he was a good four or five years younger than me. Sadly, I could see the apprehension on his parent's faces about what Johnny was doing, through the smiles they wore trying to disguise their concern.

It seemed as if every day there were more and more news reports filled with anti-war crap. There was little question that this was an unpopular war. In fact, in many parts of the country, a Marine or soldier would not even wear their uniform in public for fear of conflict. In San Diego, of course, it was a totally different sentiment with it being a military town and all.

Nevertheless, Frank and I were of one resolve, we were going to go to Vietnam and do our duty for our Corps and our country and not let the anti-war fervor detract us in any manner. I think we both knew that if we went to Vietnam with that mindset, we would never have a shot at making it home alive.

Frank and I talked about the impending danger that we would face many times in those 30 short days of leave. We even actually talked about getting an insurance policy on each since we figured we had a 50/50 shot at one of us not making it home. This is something we always joked about, but the truth is we both knew the profound reality of the situation at hand. We also, in our own morbid joking way, laughed about having to identify somebody quickly that had the same size feet as we did. Because if we lost our left foot, we would want to find somebody that lost their right foot, so we would only have to buy one pair of shoes and could save money by splitting the costs. Marines tend to use humor to avoid the realities of war, and as it turned out, we were no exception to this rule.

Like all good things, our 30-day leave came to an end all too quickly. I could not believe that the time had gone by so fast, but the calendar told me otherwise. It had been a fantastic time with friends, family, girls, and beers but it was time to pack our sea bags, get on the plane to Vietnam and do our duty.

My parents drove Frank and I up to Norton Air Force Base on the 26th of June 1968. We were traveling in our summer service uniforms, which consisted of a blouse (Marines use this term for an outer jacket when a shirt is worn underneath) over a shirt and tie. It was way too hot to be wearing while we were traveling to a tropical climate, but that was the uniform of the day, so that is what we were required to wear at the time. All the rest of our uniforms, including our field utilities we carried with us in sea bags along with a small amount of other personal items. You must get selective on what is essential when you pack your bags for war.

We arrived at Norton Air Force Base and went directly to the terminal where our civilian aircraft, a Continental Airlines jet, was to leave from that day. The flight, however, had been delayed for several hours, and we had no choice but to sit there and wait.

My mother didn't stop crying the entire time. Every time I would even look in her direction, she would just burst out into tears again.

Finally, I turned to Frank O'Brien and Warren Pinckert, another 2nd Lieutenant who was flying with us and whispered, "We have to get out of here and get a beer." We stealthily snuck out of the terminal on some trumped-up pretense I don't really remember and went down to the O club (Marine for Officer's club). We quickly downed a few beers and made our way back to the terminal.

Mom was still crying. My dad was quite serious about the whole affair, at one point

with a very sullen look in his eyes he turned
to me and whispered so my mom couldn't
hear him "Watch out for mortars. They're the
worst, you'll not be able to do anything about
them but hunker down". My dad was a WWII
veteran in the Pacific theater and was part of
the Marine amphibious force that invaded
Saipan. I was soon to find out how accurate
his advice about mortars actually was.

Saying goodbye to my mom was
extremely difficult for both me and Frank.
She had come to treat Frank as if he were
another son and we all knew that the chances
of one of us not coming back were high. The
flight was finally called, and I trudged down
the terminal walkway with Frank on one side
and Warren on the other listening to my
mother's cries fading in the distance. Our
13month long journey was about to begin.

CHAPTER 7
A long trip to a war zone

As we buckled into our comfortable
Continental Airlines flight from Norton
Airforce base in California on our way to
Okinawa, I looked around and noticed we
were all holding on to our orders papers
tightly. They were, of course, our first real set
of original orders printed out and given to us
at The Basic School in Quantico and initially,
we had been ordered to report to Treasure
Island in San Francisco but somewhere along
the way it was changed to Norton. Aside
from having the names of several other 2nd
Lieutenants on them, Frank O'Brien and
Warren Pinckert included, which helped
everyone know they were where they were
supposed to be, they limited our weight
endorsement to 55 pounds of baggage
making packing even more difficult than it
already was.

The flight to Okinawa took around 14
hours, and the flight attendants couldn't have

been any better at their jobs or any better looking that's for sure. We all knew that this was the last time we were going to see those beautiful round-eyed American girls for a while, so there was a lot of banter back and forth on that flight. They knew where we were going and were great about playing the game. They would even sit down on the armrest from time to time and chat. Most of them had made many trips back and forth and knew what Marines looked like going over and more importantly what they looked like coming back.

I will never forget the forlorn look in one particular stewardesses' eye as she looked at all of us. You could see the sadness in her eyes. Even though she was similar in age to most of us, she spoke to us as if she were a mother who was concerned about the well-being of her brood and awaited their safe return.

As I sat on the plane between O'Brien and Pinckert floating over an eerily moonlit ocean, I had some time to reflect. Was I really up to leading Marines in battle? What would it be like if I had to kill somebody?

107

How would I feel after? We learned a lot about how to kill in our training in Quantico, but we were never taught how to deal with the aftermath of death.

The 14-hour long flight passed rather quickly, and we were able to grab some chow and even a little shuteye during the trip before landing in Okinawa on the afternoon of June 29th, 1967. We checked in our sea bags and were informed what time to report back in the morning for our flight to Vietnam. The Marine base in Okinawa was quite expansive and had a great BOQ (Basic Officers Quarters) facilities. We immediately changed into our utilities and didn't waste a second of time before heading into Koza city where we heard there were plenty of women and bars.

We made the most of our time in Okinawa, a scant 25 hours in which we never slept, and in which I got my first "hotsy bath." Frank and I both enjoyed the company of some local Okinawan women who were quite accommodating. In fact, Frank and I crossed paths at one point during the evening when he was walking out of one room where he had been with one woman as I was walking out of a room where I had been with another. I looked at him and asked, "How was yours?" to which he replied "Great! How was yours?" and in my happy tone I replied "Great!" So, we immediately switched rooms and went for round two with each other's girls. We were soon to be brothers in combat, and we certainly saw nothing wrong with the situation given the time left before entering the actual war.

We got back to base, Camp Smith, just in time to get shaved and showered before we had to collect our gear. Much of the small amount of equipment that we brought with us was left in Okinawa to be stored for us to pick up on our way back, if we made it back was the running joke. We elected to take the bus to Fatima Air Force Base, and again I boarded a plane with O'Brien, Pinckert and several other 2nd Lieutenants, this time it was a much less luxurious military C130 rolling down the strip. It wasn't nearly as comfortable as the Continental jet we took to Okinawa, and there wasn't a stew in sight. The seats were made of netting and were

109

uncomfortable as hell. The flight took several hours, and most of us were either hung over or still drunk and either we just slept right there on the floor or "made do" and passed out on the netting seats. Eventually, we woke up as we flew into Da Nang Air Base.

CHAPTER 8

DA NANG ME!

As we approached Vietnam and our ultimate destination of Da Nang what really struck me most was the lushness of the land. The coastline seemed picturesque, and from my aerial point of view, it looked like the perfect vacation spot. My opinion on that, however, would change...rapidly!

We landed in Da Nang at 0700 in the morning on June 30th, 1967. The landing was a welcome end to an uncomfortable last leg of our journey to war. I can honestly say I'm not sure there is anything less comfortable than flying as a passenger on a vintage Marine Corps C130 with a hangover.

We taxied into the terminal and disembarked from our uncomfortable journey, grumpy and hungover. We trudged off the plane to the faces of dozens of Marines who were waiting to board the very plane we were leaving behind. As I looked over their faces, what I saw were not the

Marines I was used to seeing. Most of them looked haggard, thin, and just plain tired. But it wasn't physical tiredness that I saw in their eyes, it was a tiredness of the soul and a general lack of emotion. They all seemed to have a look on their faces of stark disbelief that they had actually survived and were about to go home.

In what seemed like an odd trade of the new for the weary no words were said between us officers disembarking from the plane and those waiting on the tarmac. They were an eerily quiet group for Marines, no singing, no joking around...no laughter at all. Just a collective anxiousness to board the newly arrived C130 and get the hell out of Vietnam. If you asked me how to describe this group of fellow Marines, I could only say they all appeared to be dirty, grubby, and tanned. All these years later I can still see their faces, and I would soon understand why they had that look in their eyes. It's a look that can only be placed on your soul by the stain of war, and although the stain may fade over time, nothing can ever indeed remove that kind of darkness.

All the Marines from the inbound C130 flight were assigned to 1st Marine Division. There were a few Captains sprinkled in with the 2nd Lieutenants from my Basic School class and after a short wait we were all bussed over to 1st Marine Division Headquarters where we were hit with the standard Marine Corps hurry up and wait.

We were told that we would be meeting with the Commanding General of the 1st Marine Division, General Robinson, but he would not be on site until the next day, so we would have to stand fast. We were also informed that we would have a lecture and briefing on the M16 which we had briefly been introduced to back at The Basic School in Quantico. It seemed that even though we had just completed training on the M14 that command was intent on us transitioning to the M16.

Warren Pinckert, Frank O'Brien, and I were still together, and we were all assigned to the same hooch (Marine for a tent) on our first night in Da Nang. We caught some scuttlebutt about a Naval Officers' Club in Da Nang that we could take a taxi or a tuk-tuk too quickly. So of course, not knowing what to expect the next day, we went as fast as we could get out of there. We had a delicious steak dinner that night for $2.25 which even for the time was unbelievably cheap for Vietnam or anywhere in the world really. We were still in the grubby utilities that we had flown in from Okinawa in, and it was interesting to note that the Navy and Air Force Officers at the club were all neat and clean and wore regular uniforms instead of utilities. We, of course, took great pride in standing out from the other branches of the military even though we were just newbies to Vietnam.

The next day we had a briefing from General Robinson, a tall, gray-haired, stately looking gentleman. Who I would find out was actually good friends with my father. The details of which I would learn much more about later.

The briefing, luckily, was conducted in an airconditioned room which was crowded with 2nd Lieutenants and the few Captains who had arrived with us the day prior. We then went out and fired the M16 inside the wire at a makeshift range by the division CP and had a brief lecture on it to follow up after the shoot.

The one thing everyone in Vietnam could agree on in a time of war was that it was hot, unbelievably hot and the humidity just made it worse. We were continually sucking down salt pills, sweating our butts off and my canteen practically became a part of my hand. In the next 13 months, I would see more than one Marine drop from dehydration and find myself on the edge of dehydration several times as well.

We were all called in to receive our assignments, and I will never forget walking across the hill where the 1st Marine Division was located and hearing music floating through the air out of an enlisted Marine GP tent. It stopped me cold in my tracks. It was the last song I had heard as I left the States. It was "Groovin" by The Young Rascals. I can still remember the words floating out over the hillside "Groovin on a Sunday afternoon. Feeling I couldn't get away too soon.". What I remember most about that moment and what still comes back to me as I think about it today was how hard I was struck by the incongruity of hearing that song in San Diego and then hearing it in a battle zone in Vietnam. The meaning behind the song had changed with the location and situation I was in. I have always looked at the music I listened to as the soundtrack of my life as I am sure many of you do. This song will forever be on my top ten list for the profoundness it had to me on this day.

Pinckert, O'Brien and I were all assigned to the 7th Marine Regiment that day and later we were trucked out to Hill 55 along with two other Lieutenants and taken to the 7th Marine Regiment Command Post. We still did not have weapons, and we all felt incredibly uncomfortable being in a combat zone without at least a pistol on our side. As we drove to Hill 55, the landscape and attitude changed with every passing mile. Closer to Da Nang people waved to us and appeared to be friendly but as Da Nang faded in the rearview, we saw fewer and fewer people, and when we did, they would seldom wave, even the countryside seemed less friendly.

Upon arrival at the Regimental CP, we received a briefing on the current state of things for the Regiment and a bit of low down on troops and locals. Pinckert, O'Brien and I were then faced with the decision as to whether or not we were to go to 1st Battalion 7th Marines or 2nd Battalion 7th Marines. 1st Battalion it seemed, needed two 2nd Lieutenants, and 2nd Battalion needed one.

I turned to Frank and said "Frank, your choice. Do you want the 1st Battalion or 2nd Battalion?". Frank opted for 2nd Battalion, so I was left with 1st Battalion. The 1st Battalion was based on Hill 55, and the 2nd

117

Battalion was based on another hill across the river. Frank departed that day for his new Battalion. Pinckert and I stayed behind and were soon informed that we would not be assigned to our companies or pick up our platoons until we had attended the Land Mine and Boobytrap School.

The words hit me hard as they seemed so foreign to my life up to that point. Yes, we knew there would be landmines and booby traps in Vietnam but the fact there was an entire school based on this was just another unrealistic reminder of where we were, what we had gotten into and how the odds of surviving this ordeal intact were not in our favor. We left for Land Mine and Boobytrap School the next morning.

CHAPTER 9
Hill 55
An introduction to war

Land Mine and Booby Trap School was probably the best two days of schooling I have ever attended. It obviously saved countless lives and without question saved my life multiple times. We learned some excellent scoop (Marine for knowledge) while going through Land Mine and Booby Trap School and I am sure Pinckert felt the same as I did and hoped the training would pay off. However, I must confess I had an overwhelming feeling of dread that it would be hard to spend my 13 months in Vietnam and altogether avoid getting hit by a booby trap or land mine as it seemed to be increasingly common in the war. Frankly, I was almost resigned to the fact I might lose a leg.

With the knowledge of what could happen, I made up my mind, right then and there. Whatever was going to happen, was

119

going to happen and aside from being as vigilant as possible and keeping my men on their toes there was little more, I could do. I made my peace and accepted the fact that the area of operation for the 7th Marine Regiment was the worst in the entire Marine Corps regarding land mines and booby traps. The 1st Marine Engineer Battalion ran the Land Mine and Booby Trap School, and it was quite posh in comparison to Hill 55. I mean hey they had showers with running water. Strange how circumstance can dictate luxury.

I managed to pick up some jungle boots (in that climate jungle boots can save you a lot of pain) and other clothes left behind by a Marine Captain, and as luck would have it, he was a size 12 boot. Not quite my size 13 but they fit, and I wasn't going to look a gift horse in the mouth. Anytime you could grab gear that made life easier we would do it because we were never properly outfitted and generally had to fend for ourselves.

The other benefit of going to the Land Mine and Booby Trap school was we got to go out drinking in Da Nang three nights in a row. The club was excellent, although a significant change from the Beachcomber in San Diego, and as luck would have it, there was air conditioning and entertainment as well. Two of the three nights they had a big breasted German gal singing and dancing and she definitely got our attention.

We got a bit of free time during our couple of days at the Landmine and Booby Trap School, so I took advantage of the situation and went for a run. My goal was to stay in the best shape possible so I could stay up with my troops when I finally picked up my Platoon. Little did I know how tough that was going to be. It is one thing to run in shorts, and a completely different beast to hump it through the jungle with all your equipment in the searing heat and devastating humidity of Vietnam. It was also quite odd and uncomfortable for me to be running without a weapon in a theater of combat.

As the school progressed, we dug up and disarmed dummy booby traps and uncovered, identified, and marked land mines. The instructors were very skilled at their jobs and did not hesitate to let us know in graphic

121

detail what would happen to us if we were ever hit by one of these obstacles. I am sure I wasn't the only one but the entire school I could not shake the feeling that I would get hit by one during my time in Vietnam. I just hoped it wouldn't be too bad when I did. It was tough to do a tour in Vietnam as a grunt (Marine for…well, Marine) and not pick up a Purple Heart and I had somewhat resigned myself to that fact although I had also promised myself, I would do everything I could to avoid that fate.

We didn't talk about it much outside of jokes which were really just a coping mechanism, but we thought about death a lot. At least I did, and I am sure Pinckert did as well. But I felt that I had lived a good life thus far and I was a Marine, fighting for the American cause in Vietnam and I did not allow myself to complain. None of us did, as we knew it would serve no purpose and only bring doubt.

Watching some of the Privates and PFC's going through the school I couldn't help but feel sorry for them. These were 18, and 19-year-old boys with minimal life experience and many of them were going to die young. Seeing them and knowing many of them would die was hard. I was only a few years older than most of them, and that thought rang right to me, but I realized it was ultimately a price we would have to pay.

I was sick and tired by this point of hearing all the bullshit antiwar rhetoric of how we were wrong and shouldn't be fighting in Vietnam. I had heard it every day while I was attending the University of California at Berkeley and read it in the newspapers every day since. I felt we had to see the war through, or America could never again raise its head proudly and proclaim itself the defender of democracy and a guardian of the oppressed. Was that thought stream a little too altruistic? Maybe, but I was a patriot at my very core and felt that America needed to make a stand in Vietnam, and it was our duty to fight the spread of communism throughout the world on every front.

Going over my war diaries from my time in Vietnam it struck me that I took time to note these feelings. In fact, on July 3rd, 1967,

123

one day before our great nation's celebration of our own independence, instilled with an extra sense of patriotism I'm sure, I made a note of our country's incredible heritage. How it to me was such a beautiful thing and how it gave me strength to know that the hardships we were enduring here in Vietnam had been suffered by Americans before.

I wrote quite a bit in my diary on that day. I noted "One war does not protect democracy forever and we must be prepared to fight again and again. We have to stand up and defend ourselves against those who feel democracy is weak and corrupt." And continued my observation with "Those who think they can sit back on their fat ass and wake up to a rosy world every morning with a fully stocked refrigerator, fast food on every corner, cold booze, big cars and all the trappings of modern life do not face up to reality." I wrote further that: "If we want to keep the good things in life for posterity, then we must be prepared to sacrifice, fight and yes maybe even die for that cause."

I wrote a lot back then. Who knows, maybe it was the constant sense of impending doom to come or just the disconnect from home, but it made me want to put it all down on paper just in case. That last day of Land Mine and Booby Trap School I can remember writing my first letter home. It was to a girl named Donna who I had only met the day prior to leaving for Vietnam. We met on the beach in San Diego. She was a Pi Phi at San Diego State and was a stunning woman who really filled out a bikini well. I remember thinking that this was going to be my last day in the rear (Marine for a safe non-combat zone) and it may be my last chance to get out a letter for a while or maybe ever if I was honest with myself.

The next day we reported back to Hill 55 and Battalion Headquarters where the Battalion 3 (Marine for operations officer) briefed us on what we could expect. I was assigned to Delta Company on July 6th, 1967 and took over command of the 2nd Platoon.

Our Company Commander was 1st Lieutenant Reneau who seemed pleasant enough initially but later proved to be an absolute monster and a complete failure as a leader. He was without a doubt the worst Marine officer I ever served with.

My Platoon Sergeant who had been the acting Platoon Commander was a Staff Sergeant by the name of Malone. Our company was based on Hill 55 and charged with defending the Regimental Command Post as well as the Battalion Headquarters which was also located on Hill 55.

Hill 55 was located in a very strategic location. It was low lying and about one and a half miles long and, in some areas, almost three-quarters of a mile wide. There were little knolls everywhere and fingers that spurred out from the hill. The road from Da Nang went right through Hill 55 and descended on the southern side across the Hill 55 road bridge which crossed the La Tho River. There were still remnants of old French bunkers left on Hill 55 (as well as other hills in the area) from the First Indochina War which ended in July of 1954.

Hill 55 had a mess hall where troops coming in from the field could get a nice hot meal. There was an artillery battery of 105's as well that supported out field operations. Even though the hill was only located eight miles from Da Nang, it seemed like it was already a lifetime away. The bridge on the south side of Hill 55 that crossed the La Tho river was absolutely vital to communications and resupply of all Marine units to the south, in particular, the Arizona area. This was the bridge on which a few weeks later I would spend the worst night One day I went on a patrol with corporal Evans's squad of my life. Stopping at a river, I broke out a map as I was unsure of our exact location. Evans was a short black outstanding squad leader. Evans was on my left. Suddenly, after looking at the map a shot rang out from across the river. Evans was shot through the right shoulder and dropped to the ground. I grabbed a hold of him and pulled him over the berm of the rice paddy with bullets spraying all around us. I asked Evans if he was OK, and he responded: "Sir, this is my third "purp"and I'm going home. This would not be the first time that I would hear this comment. I was lucky that day. It was obvious that shot was meant for me and the sniper had pulled the trigger to hard sending the round into Evans shoulder. Luck it seems was on my side that day.

Pulling him further back into some bushes oh, I asked him if he could walk. He said he could because it was too dangerous to call in a medevac with a sniper in an ambush across the river. He managed to walk out to an area where we could safely call in a helicopter medivac.

I learned a lot from Evans as I did from my other squad leaders. I will never forget a day early on after taking over the platoon when I sent one man across a rice paddy, I did not want to risk two or more men. That was what we were taught at the Basic School. After the patrol was over Evans asked me, very respectively, if he could speak to me in private. I of course, said yes. He said, Very respectfully, that I should not ever send one marine alone but always send two at least. We are more confident and marines are used to working with another marine. It made sense to me and I followed his advice thereafter.

It was a difficult task taking over Delta Company 2nd Platoon. They had all already seen weeks if not months of combat duty, and I didn't know the names of anyone in the

Platoon. I introduced myself to the squad leaders separately then called the Platoon together in an informal pow wow kind of setting to introduce myself as their new Platoon Commander.

I knew nothing about the backgrounds of my men yet or even what experience they had individually. I could see almost instantly by the looks on their faces that there was a complete sense of distrust and disbelief that a brand new fresh out of OCS 2nd Lieutenant was going to be leading them. Being a "Boot Luey" may be the most challenging job in the Marine Corps. Nobody has faith in you up or down the ladder of rank, and you must prove yourself with every decision no matter how small or large. Which in the rear may not mean much, but in the field, during combat could cost a life or in fact several lives.

Unlike Marine units today who go to battle as a unit that has trained together, we had individual replacements in Vietnam which was a huge mistake.

A unit that trains together before combat will be more efficient in a combat situation. Many of us who remained in the Marine Corps after the war took the position that only units, not individuals, should be rotated into combat situations whenever possible. Thankfully the Marine Corps has gone to unit rotations whenever possible.

Shortly after my somewhat awkward introduction the company gunny took me down to the company area and introduced me around. He grabbed a flak jacket from a wounded Marine who was being evacuated to the hospital in the rear. It was covered in fresh blood and was handed to me without a word of apology or a second thought to its state. This I would find out was pretty much SOP, you got gear when and where you could get it in Vietnam. I was happy to have it, blood-soaked or not, and even though I would soon come to hate wearing it in the sweltering heat of Vietnam, I knew it was a pathway to possible survival. The blood didn't really bother me to tell you the truth, it was just another part of a dirty flak jacket as far as I was concerned.

CHAPTER 10
My First Patrol

The very next day after I met my new platoon, I went out on what would be my first patrol in Vietnam. I let the squad leader take lead on the patrol which I came into the practice of doing if I went out with only a squad size patrol. I didn't want to take away the authority of the squad leader over his men when we only had his squad on hand.

The villages we went through were not a pleasant sight, it was like nothing I had ever seen. You hear scuttlebutt and stories, but nothing fully prepares you for that kind of culture shock. It was a strange mix of new sights. It wasn't uncommon to come across a random Buddha in the jungle in the vicinity of the villages and the villages themselves were like nothing I had seen before.

The kids were full of sores and disease. Often pleading to us for food since the VC would take most of theirs for their troops. Toddlers of two and three years old whose eyes were closed shut with sores due to infection. We thought many of them were blind, but a corpsman told me it was simply because the mothers never washed the sand from their eyes. So, I asked him to clean their eyes out and when he did the kids seemed incredulous that they could actually see the world. Some for the first time it seemed.

The women in the villages all chewed "betel nut" which made their teeth a blackish brown color. It in fact I would learn, was fruit from the Areca palm that grows widely in

133

Southern Asia and Eastern Africa that has a slightly psychoactive ingredient called arecoline that is similar to nicotine in tobacco and much like tobacco is now known to be highly carcinogenic. There were no young men in the villages, but there were plenty of pregnant women. The villages were generally surrounded by rice paddies and then there was jungle.

Our patrol routes were dictated by the Battalion S-3 based on intel and suspected enemy activity. This patrol had six checkpoints in total and at each checkpoint the patrol leader would check in with battalion. Luckily this patrol went pretty much without incident, and we took no fire. However, we did shoot at one man who wouldn't stop when we ordered him to (which I would come to find out meant he was most likely VC) but he was able to get away from us and hide in the jungle. I quickly learned as well that any younger men in the area were also assumed to be VC and shot on sight.

I was determined to follow the training I had gotten at OCS as we were told again and again it would save our lives and the men teaching us were seasoned Marines who had lived through Vietnam. So of course, coming up on our first rice paddy I halted the patrol and like I was trained I sent one man across first alone in the event there was a sniper. Later that day back in base camp I would learn two incredibly important lessons about Vietnam. First, you can learn a lot from your salty enlisted Marines so listen to what they say. Second never send a single Marine on a mission. If you send two the others see they always have backup and the motivation level is higher. Alone they feel like they don't matter and are nothing but a target for the enemy. Moral drops and you lose control of your command over time. Evans was the salty Marine who would teach me that important lesson and it was one I would never forget.

More than anything on this first patrol it was hot! Wearing a flak jacket, ammunition, grenades, web gear etc. in that heat just wore me down. I also had a bad case of the runs that I had picked up a couple of days before and in all caught up to me and pretty much wiped me out when we got back to Hill 55. I just sunk into a makeshift rack and prayed for it all to go away.

I not only tried to get to know my platoon but the others in the company as well as I thought all good commanders should know their supporting elements as well as their own men.

There was a tent on the hill that the officers of Delta Company used which had a wooden floor and electric lights fed by a generator further up the hill. We fashioned a makeshift shower, which was pretty much just a five-gallon bucket with some holes poked in the bottom. The troops all hung Playboy pictures in their hooch's which made it a little more difficult I thought, not being around women and all, it just made me think of them more. We also had hot chow and cold beer in the beginning so there were "field luxuries" that helped us keep up morale. Many of these luxuries on Hill 55 would quickly become things of the past.

I had hardly eaten anything the last few days and the heat just sucked any strength I had out of me. It was physically the most complex thing I had ever done to that point and although I stuck it out like a true Marine, I found out later that I had suffered from heat exhaustion. Luckily after two days I was back to normal and settled in quite nicely.

CHAPTER 11
This is Real Combat

July 10th, 1967! For every person on this planet there are days in their lives they want to remember and conversely days in their lives they most likely want to forget. July 10th, 1967 is a day in my life that I will never forget. July 10th, 1967 was my first real day of combat!

I took out my entire platoon on patrol that day, not just a single squad and the patrol lasted pretty much the entire day. We always had checkpoints along the patrol route and would stop and report to command at each checkpoint. Pretty basic SOP for a patrol and depending on the length or suspected enemy activity we would add in extra checkpoints if needed for communications and safety. Sometimes you would have five checkpoints and sometimes you could have eight or nine if the patrol warranted that level of communication. It was essentially a way to keep in contact with the battalion and assure the brass everything was going as planned.

On this particular day we actually blew two tunnels we had been advised of before the patrol and found without issue and aside from our explosive blasts to the tunnels up to that point everything had gone quietly.

As had been on the previous day, and many days to come, the villages we went through were populated only with women and children. Many of the women were obviously pregnant. There were never any males between the age of fifteen and forty-

139

five in these villages since most of them had been conscripted by the VC to fight. From time to time, we would come across an older man who was obviously too old for conscription.

The children all had the same hygiene issues with their skin and eyes and we would try to help by giving them soap to wash themselves. But they were so desperately poor they would take the soap and sell it on the black market for money or barter it for food. And like the day prior on my first squad patrol, it was crazy hot. I was still not used to the heat. And, I was still struggling with the flax jacket, extra gear, and the trots. All and all I was one seriously hurting puppy.

We reached the next to last checkpoint for the patrol and decided to take a short break. Being standard patrol SOP when we stopped as always, I had my men lay down a defensive perimeter while I checked in with command on the radio.

I was still getting to know the men in my platoon, and I am sure that while many of them appreciated the break in the patrol, many just wanted to keep moving and get back to the CP so they could take off their gear and cool down. I would say the average age of my Marines when I took over the platoon was 18. Although most of them looked much younger and some probably were. Strangely though at this point in my service even being the older more worldly man I was still the "boot" (Marine for new guy) and they were the salty (Marine for experienced) ones.

We got all our Corpsmen (the only Navy guys Marines give no shit to) from battalion and we had just received a new one about the same time I came on board. These Corpsmen didn't come into the country with us but would come in on Naval flights from their particular schools and then be assigned to us from battalion. Each platoon would have two corpsmen at any given time.

I was carrying an M16 along with my .45 colt 1911 as I wanted to try and look like every other man in my platoon and not stand out as an officer that some sniper might think was worth taking a shot at. In retrospect though it would have been quite obvious to anyone watching that I was in charge since I was the one barking out orders and calling in on the radio to command.

As we started to move out from our checkpoint, this new Corpsman stepped in the patrol formation in front of me and I, for some reason, did not say or do anything to get him in place toward the rear end of the patrol group which would be his usual position since Corpsman are there primary to

142

patch up the wounded and traditionally only carry a .45 Colt 1911.

We hadn't gone more than a few hundred meters after stepping out when shots rang out. We were taking enemy fire for the first time since I had been in charge. The Corpsman in front of me went down with a wound through his leg just above the knee. He was screaming and bleeding like a stuck pig and obviously in quite a lot of pain.

My platoon, as salty as they were, took up defensive positions and returned fire. I dropped down to a low crawl position and crawled toward the Corpsman with rounds landing all around me. Suddenly there were strange thoughts dancing in my head that I could not suppress. I was thinking about Rudyard Kipling's poem "Gunga Din" where the poem reads:

When 'e went to tend the wounded under fire!
It was "Din! Din! Din!"
With the bullets kickin' dust-spots on the green.
When the cartridges ran out,

143

☐ You could hear the front-files shout,
☐ "Hi! ammunition-mules an' Gunga Din!"

The bad guys were now concentrating on me now since I was the one barking out the orders. I could see the dust from the bullets hitting the ground all around me.

I also strangely wondered why this individual was shooting at me since I was a really nice guy. I thought, "If he knew me better, he wouldn't want to hurt me because he would like me" . Strange thoughts to say the least with all the firing going on around me.

My Marines however had my back and were shooting back at the ambush while I treated the Corpsman's wounds and applied a tourniquet. Thinking to myself the entire time I did "What's wrong with this picture? I'm treating the Corpsman who should be treating me." After all, he had stepped in front of me where he should not have been. It was obvious, at least to me, that the VC who shot the Corpsman thought he was the platoon commander and was not aware our column positions had been reversed.

144

After recovering from the surrealism of Rudyard Kipling running through my mind and applying a tourniquet and compress to the wounded Corpsman's leg. I had my radioman call in to battalion for a medevac helicopter.

I then had to formulate how we were going to get out of this ambush because we were pinned down behind a dike wall. There were dike walls and rice paddies everywhere in Vietnam.

With a clear head I was able to focus on action and crawled down to the fire team on my left flank. We were all jammed up together against the dike wall. I yelled to the rest of the platoon to lay down a base of fire. When they did, I took the fire team and advanced across the open space (never had I run that fast before) to the tree line where the firing was coming from. Leap frogging one by one laying down cover fire as we advanced on the enemy position.

Rounds were hitting all around us and I was absolutely stunned that I was not getting hit and neither were my men. A small miracle with all the rounds coming down range our

145

way. We finally reached the tree line and did a quick reconnoiter of the area but found no VC in the area. It seems that as soon as they realized we had enveloped their position they ran off into the neighboring jungle.

All of a sudden, a wave of exhaustion came over me. I had been so focused on tending to the downed Corpsman and then firing my rifle continuously at the enemy that I didn't notice my own body telling me back off. I thought for sure I was about to pass out, but I wasn't about to let that happen and embarrass myself in front of my new platoon. It was 125 degrees that day and we had been out for four hours of intense crawling, running, and searching for VC. I wasn't used to it yet and that damn flak jacket was determined to do me in.

After securing the area we finally got a medevac helicopter in to get the wounded Corpsman out of the field and to a hospital. Thankfully, battalion sent some tanks out shortly afterward as we were making our way back to base camp at Hill 55. They picked us up and drove us most of the short distance back, which was a great relief to me because

146

I wasn't sure I would have made it back humping in that heat.

I learned a valuable lesson that day at the expense of that Corpsman. Every man has his place in a patrol formation, and nobody changes places without my okay. However, I am forever grateful that the Corpsman made that mistake that day. Had he not chosen to take that position in front of me, had I not been new to the field, it would have been a short-lived existence for me in Vietnam. The leg wound was quite bad, and we never saw that Corpsman again.

The one thing about being at war that you can't get away from is that war doesn't follow a clock. It's not a nine to five job. War doesn't have a time clock or a meditation corner. There is no place to relax and take it easy in a combat zone. It is a twenty-four-hour seven day a week job that is 99.9% boredom and .01% absolute fucking terror.

The very next day we were sent out to lay barbed wire around a footbridge which was on a finger that jutted out from Hill 55. The foot bridge crossed over a river on the east side of Hill 55 which was real Indian country. Indian country was our reference to heavily protected enemy area that was dangerous at any time.

I am positive that some of my men gained confidence in me that day and possibly thought I was the smartest Marine that ever lived when I remembered something I had been taught back at The Basic School about how to lay barbed wire on top of a preexisting layer of barbed wire.

The barbed wire was in coils you see and to get the coils to lay on top of each other it was important to bounce a coil and specifically to get it bouncing in rhythm. It was almost a combat version of ballet if you will. We would get the coil bouncing with several Marines holding it on either side then on the high arc of the bounce we would lift and place it on top of the other coil. This would nicely settle in and form a nice barrier.

My Marines had been struggling with how to do this effectively because if you just tried to lift it up and set it on top the barbs would catch and make a cluster fuck of wire. When I showed them this trick, I had learned back in The Basic School they were amazed at how easy it was and not only got it done but they had some fun with it. I got positive feedback from them proclaiming "Good going Lieutenant! Good going!". At least maybe they thought now I wasn't some dumb ass green 2nd Lieutenant and maybe I had some smarts. Well, I was hoping that was what they were thinking anyway.

CHAPTER 12
Little GTO

On July 11th we moved off Hill 55 and headed north to a key bridge named Duong Lam. One of the other battalions was going on an operation, and we had been charged with securing the bridge for a few days in their absence.

This is when I would meet GTO for the first time. GTO was my first real contact and time spent getting to know a Vietnamese person. He lived in a little village close by Duong Lam bridge. The bridge itself was about two miles from Hill 10 which I would become very familiar with soon.

The locals around this bridge and particularly from GTO's village were very friendly people. They were anti-communist and quite pacified as far as the local population went. They had their own defense force but relied upon us heavily for protection against the VC.

The bridge was old, really old, and the bunkers we utilized were poorly laid out, just like the bunkers in the defensive positions just south of Hill 55. This bridge and the village and people who surrounded it were to become a sort of safe haven for us Marines as we would come to find out very soon.

In the village was a group of young boys that ran around like wild Indians, but it didn't take long before I realized that there was a natural leader to that wild bunch, a young boy we would eventually nickname GTO. I would watch them run around and he would bark out orders at them and generally keep them in line.

The Marines started to call the young leader GTO because he knew all the words to the song "Little GTO" by Ronnie and the Daytona's. He would, with a little prompting from us, often break into a very animated version of the song in broken English and without fail punctuated by a myriad of swear words. It was quite the site and we had a lot of fun laughing at his presentation.

He was either eleven or twelve years old when we first met. The Vietnamese used a different calendar system, so it was a bit of a cultural and mathematical difference when it came to trying to figure out birth dates. No matter what age he was though he could already swear as bad as any Marine and "Mother Fucker" ended almost every one of his sentences.

After we assessed the bridge area and determined that it was relatively secure, I asked GTO to ride his bike alongside me and carry my .45 Colt 1911 while I went on a short two-mile run. In retrospect it was stupid of me to go on that run. The VC would have loved to either capture or shoot a young 2nd Lieutenant running along a path in shorts and boots without his platoon around to support him.

The entire time we were on the bridge, GTO was by my side each and every day. He even washed my uniform for me in the river if I gave him my hand soap. My guess is he wanted to take a bath himself and washing the clothes was a way to get soap. Initially though, I would not let him inside the wire at night because it was strictly against Division orders to have a foreign national inside and I was new to the unit and didn't really know what rules we could bend.

As I have mentioned the defenses on the bridge were poor to say the least. The

154

bunkers had been poorly positioned and were falling to pieces. The wire around the perimeter itself was also inadequate and those factors coupled with the fact that I was marginally understrength to properly defend such a position to me was a recipe for failure. I should have had 40 men on that bridge to be at proper strength, but the fact was my platoon would never reach that strength the entire time I was in Vietnam.

Nights on the bridge were rough. We were on 100 percent alert every night and it was my responsibility as Platoon Commander to make sure all my Marines were awake and alert. It seemed like every night we would get word someone was going to get hit.

I got chewed out by some random Marine Major for letting some of my men be on the bridge without helmets and boots. I had my men go without boots whenever possible . They wore flip-flops instead. He was more upset about the fact that he had not been saluted. I explained to him that we did not salute officers crossing the bridge because we did not want them to become a target.

But it didn't stop me from touring the line several times to make sure everyone was awake and on point. It was absolutely necessary to keep checking the men in their foxholes at night. The old policy of shooting anyone who fell asleep on watch was crap from the past if you asked me. Men were up days at a time in sweltering heat and could fall asleep at a moment's notice. (Little known fact: Marines can sleep anytime, anywhere in any position) To me it was just part of mine and my Platoon Sargent's duty to help the men stay awake and alert. Plus, it was a great opportunity for me to get to know the men better and assess their confidence levels in not only myself but the unit. I was nervous about Charles lighting up that bridge, but I never let on to the men.

July 15th I was awoken from my sleep at about 0020 hours when two loud "Whoom" sounds raced overhead. It seemed that about 2500 meters from our position Charlie (most likely regular NVA) fired rockets into Da Nang. I quickly sprung too and took a defensive position just in time to see Da Nang light up like a fireball. The radio came to life with chatter requesting a pinpoint on the rockets launch position. We did our best to locate them as accurately as possible and then let the Artillery do its work.

They dropped rounds on the suspected position as surrounding units started taking fire in what seemed to be a diversionary tactic. We were even targeted with a box mine placement about 200 meters downstream from us (hoping to take out a patrol) but the mine was pointed out by one

157

of the local civilians. A man who I had paid respects to the night before by pulling a barbed wire stake from his father's grave and repositioning it elsewhere. So, he returned the favor by giving us that information and at least one Marine's life was saved that night due to his actions.

Battalion also required that while we were manning a defense on the bridge, we send four Marines each night to what was known as a CAP unit (Combined Action Program) which was close to GTO's village. The Marine Corps had formed CAP units to protect the local villages from the VC. Basically, they consisted of a squad of Marines that worked with the Popular Force (a sort of Vietnamese National Guard) to secure the villages. The CAC program was immensely successful in Vietnam and it is still my belief had the Army followed along with that program as well we would have had a far different result overall during the war.

The crappy part about the CAC was that it left me with a total strength of 21 each night on the bridge. Well short of what we required to properly secure the bridge. Not to

mention that that number included two
Corpsmen, two Radiomen, my Platoon
Sergeant and myself. This was nowhere close
to being a TO platoon which is 45 men strong
and the Marine Corps standard. I would have
been happy with 30, a number I would still
never see.

I got about three hours of sleep after the
sun came up on July 15th. Seeing the sun
come up in Vietnam was always a good sight.
It meant you could mentally tick off one

more day and you were that much closer to going home. I took out a long patrol that day with no contact again. It was not surprising to have no contact with the enemy in this area since most of the people in the area around this particular bridge leading to Da Nang were very pro-government and pacified.

We would even see young men working in the rice paddies which was rare elsewhere. Still, we never truly knew who the VC was actually and who was not. So, it was always a concern when crossing big rice paddies (which were everywhere) and would sometimes take some creative encouragement on my part to get the troops moving across those paddies. But I must emphasize the fact here that, to the man, they followed orders and put their lives on the line daily.

Amid our time on Duong Lam bridge a wave of loneliness struck me. You see we were very close to Da Nang which meant we were closer to getting our mail and it came more frequently. It soon seemed like everyone was getting letters from home but me. I must explain to you the meaning of a letter in combat for you to truly understand the gravity.

Getting a letter from "the real world" when you're in a combat zone is a literal life saver. The depression of war weighs heavy on the mind of a soldier or Marine every second of every day you are there. You can quickly find yourself drowning in sorrow and self-pity if you are not careful. It messes with your head in ways you can't imagine, causes lack of sleep, doubt in yourself, in your skills, depression and a general sense of malaise. There are things that help fight against this mental aspect of war. PT, cards, shooting your rifles into the river, beer…lots of beer. All these things help band-aid the emotion for a while, but a letter from home is like a life raft in the middle of that ocean of self-doubt. It's tangible proof that someone out in the real-world cares for you and lifts your morale more than any other thing you can do for yourself.

But I still wasn't getting any letters and it was getting to me. So, getting a letter from home became a priority for me. I couldn't wait to hear something, anything, from

someone outside of the war zone. So, I
started writing letters to every woman I ever
knew in the hope that one of them would
write back.

Our days on the Duong Lam bridge were
spent cleaning our weapons and firing them
into the river when we weren't out on patrol.
Despite GTO, his gang of cohorts and
the incredibly nice people from the village, I
couldn't wait to get off that bridge. The
sitting around and waiting to be hit really
pissed me off. I would rather have been out
there hunting down Charlie than being a
sitting duck. Finally, after six days we left
Duong Lam bridge and went back to our
position on Hill 55, leaving behind GTO and
his gang. We would see each other again,
many times over the years and remain friends
for life.

CHAPTER 13
Operations Bolder Pecos & Stockton

We had only been off the Duong Lam bridge and back at Hill 55 for a few days when we got word we would be going out on an operation. In fact, the entire battalion would be going. We flew out of Hill 55 on July 20th and went down to the Arizona area where 5th Marines was located.

I knew we were there for an operation, but I had a secondary personal mission as well and immediately set out searching for Lou LeGarie. Lou was a Navy Corpsman, a friend of my father's and mine since I was 14 years old. He was an honorable man who had received a silver star at the Chosin Reservoir during the Korean War and oversaw the medical station at 5th Marines.

I met Lou when I was 14. I lived in Hawaii, one of my father's many duty stations but also one of my favorites. I was going to the Punahou School and had developed a severe ingrown toenail issue. So, Lou had me sit down in a chair while my father held my arms to my sides. Lou then held my feet between his legs and gouged out the ingrown toenails. It was extremely painful, and they bled quite a bit after, but I had always remembered Lou fondly as I did not have the problem of ingrown toenails again.

In any event, I searched the aid station and finally found Lou. It was good to see a familiar face from the past and it helped a lot just to see him. I desperately needed a new pair of trousers at the time since the crotch in mine was ripped out. Lou not only got me new trousers but a full set of utilities, found me a place with a mirror so I could actually shave while looking at what I was doing and gave me a bunch of food, including Cokes and cookies. Added sugar, how I missed you so.

Then something happened I had not quite prepared myself for during my time in training. Lou took me into a section of the aid station where a young VC or NVA soldier

165

was being roughly treated in an attempt to extract information.

He had been pretty badly wounded and had a large open wound on his chest. One of the men questioning him had inserted some sort of probe into the wound and was moving it around causing the soldier excruciating pain. It made me uncomfortable on many levels and I did not like watching it, so I got out of the tent as soon as possible.

Even though I left that area as soon as I could the images of what happened in that room have stuck with me for all these years. I regret not speaking up about the torture of the enemy soldier, but I realize also that any information obtained from him may have saved lives of Marines.

So, as I sit here today writing these words for you the reader, I know that I made the right choice, although it may seem the inhuman choice. I also know that life, while we would all like to believe it is very black and white, it has many grey areas, and sometimes the decisions we make can be right and wrong simultaneously. Which is pretty much how you boil down any war and even the Marine Corps itself. No Marine wants to go to war. No Marine wants to kill. But every Marine wants to fight for a better world, for those who cannot stand up themselves.

We as Marines live constantly in a world where you must make those grey decisions, often in real time with lives hanging in the balance. We know they may lead to things we don't necessarily agree with on a human level, yet we make those hard choices for those who do not want to live in that grey world. This is the position every soldier or Marine puts themselves in when they take their oath and they do it for their family, friends, and country. They do it because they want to stand up to those who would push people down. Not just Americans but the people of the world we share. This is what a true Marine is at their core. I am proud to have been a leader of these Devil Dogs every day and will proudly call myself Marine until the day I die.

The next morning, we lifted off for the operation which was called "Boulder Pecos". The operation would take place in Happy

Valley (a misnomer if ever there were one) which we would all wind up calling "Leech Valley" since it seemed leeches were its primary occupants.

Most of us lived in mortal fear of getting a leech up our penis and at least one man in the battalion did, during the operation, causing him to be medivaced out in the middle of the night screaming his lungs out. Which of course was not only horrific for him but put us all in great danger from the enemy.

We loaded up on CH46's for the trip to Happy Valley not really knowing what to expect. Before we even lifted off, I remember the Crew Chief of the 46 cautioning me to tell my men to be careful with their M16's when they got out of the bird because he didn't want any of the windows to get knocked out. All I could think was, "how the hell could that even happen?".

My platoon had been assigned 90 percent of the 360-degree defensive perimeter in our landing zone. A big responsibility for sure but we were ready for action and we were the first wave into the zone.

I ordered my men to follow me and I led them off the helicopter as soon as they touched down. My adrenaline was really pumping as we stood up to disembark the bird and I promptly knocked out the window behind me as I stood up to charge out the door (So that is how it happens!) into the almost eye high elephant grass. But quickly saw a wide area that had been cleared out by, what I learned later, was "Agent Orange"

It was difficult to set up our section of the perimeter defense properly as there were areas that were completely open but also a considerable amount of tall elephant grass that made eyeline communication almost impossible in our 90-degree section of the perimeter. I had to get them assembled and then deploy them into the perimeter while tying into the other platoons on our left and right flanks and it took some adjusting to make it happen, but we finally managed to do it.

It was hot, we were covered with mud and cuts from the elephant grass. My radioman got a workout that day for sure. Keep in mind that the radioman must stay with the platoon commander, at all times, no matter what!

We would later learn that the area had been sprayed with Agent Orange just prior to our landing. Many members of my platoon, including myself, were to suffer from the effects of Agent Orange in later life.

The area of operation for Boulder Pecos was surrounded by mountains. It was raining that day as we deployed on the valley floor. It was a dumb place to drop us in and we all felt like we were D&B (Marine for fucked!). D&B is a reference to the battle of Dien Bien Phu, a battle during the first Indochina War in which the Viet Minh defeated the French by completely surrounding them and bombarding them with artillery and cutting off their supply drops. This was very similar to that battle in the fact that we had put ourselves in the same type of situation by setting up our perimeter in a valley surrounded by mountains. But it was what it was, and we had to find a way to overcome the situation if we wanted to survive.

While it was not that cold temperature-wise, we would freeze at night since we were so hot during the day. We would get soaked in the rain and swelter in the heat and humidity and when the sun went down, we would freeze. I guess training in Quantico's freezing winter did have some benefits after all.

We dug in deep once we set our perimeter, knowing that we were susceptible to artillery and mortar attack, and after a night of freezing in the rain we put up some makeshift overhead cover using our ponchos. We also took our C-ration boxes and made a floor in our foxholes, so we had some footing, which was slightly better than standing in mud and water.

Battalion had set up a 105 battery at best 100 meters behind our position. They were so close that when they fired, we had to get into our foxholes to avoid the shockwaves and any foreign materials that came flying our way. If you have never been close to large artillery rounds going off, they do create quite a hefty shockwave and if you're in front of them they tend to catch dirt, small rocks and debris and send it flying outward. The possibility of losing an eye to debris was very real.

We did not have barbed wire outside of our perimeter but there was a small stream that ran below us which would make it more difficult for the enemy to advance. We were prepared for anything, but again it was not an ideal place to be sitting in a defensive perimeter.

After we got set up and tied in, I took my unit out on patrol. It was tense and slow going due to the terrain and every half an hour or so I would have to have my men stop, partner up and inspect each other for leeches. Not just a "hey do you have leeches" inspection but a detailed inspection of each man's body. You see, you can't feel a leech attach to you, as they are in the bushes and streams and when they come in contact with skin, they inject a small amount of paralytic, so you don't feel them attach. So, one man would lift his shirt and spin and then drop his trousers, spread his cheeks and lift his ball sack and penis then it was the other man's turn. Ah, the glory of war. It was relatively easy to remove them if you found one you would just dab some of the Marine Corps issued mosquito repellent on them and they would fall right off.

After the night we had to medevac out the Marine who got a leech up his penis, and I returned with part of my platoon from patrol, I had a brilliant idea. I would just dab mosquito repellent all over my private parts and that would keep any leeches from getting me where it counted most. My troops saw me doing this and all followed suit thinking it was a great idea as well. It was not! It was a slow burn and took about five minutes before it really hit me. My balls were on fire and I sprinted down to the stream to wash myself off ASAP! I was soon joined by every member of my platoon since they had all followed suit and had the same fire in their loins. If the enemy had attacked us at that point, it would have been an easy victory for them, there was literally nobody left behind to defend our positions since we were all at the stream trying to alleviate the burning. In retrospect I can sit back and laugh but at the time it was hell to pay and put us all in danger.

Back on the line I fully expected to get hit at any time. However, we never took a single round into the perimeter. Over the next few days, I took patrols all over that damn valley. It was extremely difficult finding our way around the valley. The compasses didn't work well here and the maps we did have didn't cover this area.

On our third to last day in Happy Valley, we found evidence of a lot of enemy activity. You would find areas where the brush was trodden on, and branches were broken. It is very hard for a group of men to move through the jungle and leave no trace. So, we were always on the lookout for anything of the sort. However, my platoon never spotted an enemy soldier that day.

On the last day we were out patrolling, my point man stopped and motioned me to come forward (using hand signals) indicating that he had enemy in sight looking down on a river. As I crawled toward him a small animal darted out between him and myself and my point man. This wasn't really an

174

uncommon thing to see a rodent in the bush but what happened next was.

The instant that I identified the rodent and stopped crawling forward a large black snake chasing the rodent struck out from a hidden lair in the bush and bit into the rodent then slowly withdrew back into the bush and disappeared with the rodent in its mouth. It scared the crap out of me and my point man! I froze in my tracks and watched the entire thing go down and my black point man turned ghost white watching the live action animal kingdom show. By the time we recovered, and I finally got up to my point man's position, the enemy was gone.

I went down to the river's edge to check for tracks and intel and noticed my boot size was almost the same exact size as the enemy soldier he had spotted. This was unusual since I have relatively large feet and most Southeast Asian men do not. My point man informed me however that he was a big man and apparently later in intel briefs he was identified as a Chinese man, and advisor to the NVA.

We followed the footsteps for quite a while up the riverbank hoping that we could catch him again and shoot him or capture him. I got an odd feeling after a while that something was wrong, an eerie sense of impending doom like we were about to walk into an ambush. This wouldn't be the last time I got this feeling in Vietnam. You quickly learned that when the birds stopped singing or the bugs went silent, something or someone is out there waiting. Finally, I let my senses get the best of me and I called a halt to the patrol and turned us around. I am confident that I made the right call and saved lives that day. Some days to come would not be as clear cut.

We lifted out of Happy Valley on July 27th on the way to another suspect LZ for an operation called "Stockton". This movement only involved our company, not the entire battalion, lucky us.

My platoon was sent off by itself. We moved out on a high ridge line, that later became identified as Charlie Ridge. Charlie Ridge became very well known to my platoon when we moved to Hill 41.

Initially, we couldn't find the trail and we had to cut our way through thick elephant grass using the machetes we had brought with us. It was like something out of a jungle expedition film. The men were absolutely exhausted, nothing made sense on the map, but we kept pushing on into the jungle.

Later, we discovered that we had been dropped in the entirely wrong LZ instead of our intended starting point. Which was the reason nothing made sense on the map of course. We were finally able to make contact with an AO who was overhead, and he pinpointed our location for us. We did have to pop smoke so he could spot us because the jungle was so thick.

After my platoon was sent off by itself on the second day we got rained on, or at least initially we thought it was rain. It turned out though, to not be rain at all, but in fact a sticky substance which we would later identify as Agent Orange. It had been accidentally dropped on us from our own planes. It wasn't really the tanker pilots' fault as we were not supposed to be in that location. and the jungle canopy was so thick that there was no way he could have seen us when he dropped his payload.

After the AO identified our position and we were on the trail we were supposed to be on, We were almost out of water. In my estimation, each man had less than a canteen of water. 1st Lt Reneau, our company commander, stupidly sent us off by ourselves.

The problem we had was that our rations that had been issued were dehydrated, which required water to be eaten. We were given the dehydrated rations because they did not weigh as much as the MREs. Lt Reneau should have known there would be no water on top of the ridgeline. Basically, my platoon was without food or water for almost 40 hours.

Without water for almost 40 hours and no real edible food to eat. my men were exhausted and ready to drop. My platoon was on this trail during this period of time by ourselves and I felt very uncomfortable. The reason I felt uncomfortable was that the trail we were on looked like a "highway" and there was plenty of reason to believe we would be ambushed. We later found out that the path we were on was part of the Ho Chi Minh trail on top of the ridgeline and there was plenty of evidence of enemy activity in that area.

I knew there was water down on the valley floor and I made the decision to get off the trail and get us some water. We found what looked like a trail down to the valley floor and I told my point man to take it. Later, my ass was chewed out by Reneau but I had no choice as my troops badly needed water.

About halfway down the hill we ran into a huge rockslide, which of course was not on the map. We were able to slowly crawl over the massive rocks and make our way down rock by rock, but the pace was slow going and we had to spend the night in that rocky area. Fortunately, there was a small spring running through the area, and we were able to fill up our depleted canteens and finally get some water in us. Lieutenant Reneau was extremely upset and screaming at me to get the men down to the valley floor but it was absolutely impossible to navigate the rockslide at night and survive.

On the third day of operation Stockton, we finally reached the valley floor and walked out toward the mouth of the valley, reuniting with the rest of the company. Thank goodness there were tanks and AAV's there to give us a ride the rest of the way in.

I was extremely pissed off the rest of the day for all the yelling and screaming that Reneau had done over the radio. It was overheard by many of the men and I am sure the higher ups as well and totally unnecessary for the situation. We finally walked out of the valley on July 29th and if I am completely honest, I was just happy to be out of the nightmare we had been put in.

CHAPTER 14
The Bridge on 55
& The Sappers Attack

On July 31st, 1967, after our return to Hill 55, my platoon was assigned to defend the heavily traveled bridge on a main road immediately south of Hill 55. We were afforded zero time to recover from our latest excursion into the field for operations "Stockton" and "Boulder Pecos". We were exhausted, dehydrated and could have used just a few hours of respite but when I got down to the bridge on Hill 55, I could see that there would be no rest for now.

The defensive positions on the bridge were in terrible shape. The bunkers were collapsing, and the barbed wire had grass growing in it which made it almost impossible to see any enemy that might be in the wire. I asked Reneau for additional men to help me clear the grass out or at least a flame tank to burn the grass out of the wire.

He told me no, not to do it and I will never forget his response: "I like the grass in the wire, it hides the wire from the enemy." This of course was contrary to everything we had been taught at TBS about how any grass was supposed to be at least hand grenade range outside of any wire and any defensive position. This was just one more example of his ignorance and inability to properly lead our troops. Quite frankly, by now, I had grown to hate the man. I wasn't alone in this regard, as he was disliked by most of the company.

I led a patrol out that first day on the bridge at Hill 55 and it went smoothly until

182

my point man Lance Corporal (LCPL) Sharp halted our patrol and called me up. I slowly crawled up to him and he whispered to me that he had seen movement ahead. I looked out in front of us onto what seemed to be the remains of the foundation from an old French home. This was in an area southwest of the bridge and known to be the site of a VC village.

We stared out at that house foundation for what seemed like forever, but in reality, was just a few minutes and then I saw it too, a flicker of movement cresting the remains. This was honestly what most of our patrols would boil down to, who saw who first. Tactics of course played a huge part in the battles but the luck of seeing the enemy first almost always meant an upper hand.

I called up the M60 machine gun team and had them lay down a base of suppressing fire as I sent a fire team off to my left to flank the L shaped ambush, that the VC t had set up on us. The VC ran off, we could see them running through the jungle. They got away but we hit at least one of them as we could tell by the blood trail left behind. We also captured several M79 rounds and various kinds of other ammunition.

Lance Corporal Sharp saved my life and the lives of everyone else in our squad sized patrol that day. If he had not spotted the movement (undoubtedly from his experience as a hunter growing up in Louisiana) we would have walked directly into their L shaped ambush and essentially into a kill box since there was no place to hide. The entire squad would have been killed. This would not be the last time we had trouble at this village or the last time a good point man saved my life. Good training and good execution are the true saviors on the

184

battlefield. There are no medals handed out for a point man that does his job well but maybe there should be.

The only positive thing about the day other than surviving certain death thanks to LCPL Sharp was the fact that I received three letters from home. One of them was the announcement of my sister's wedding.

August 3rd, 1967, I took out a raid patrol at 0200 to see what we could make of the area where we were ambushed. We reached the village where the L shaped ambush had been set up and quietly snuck into the village undetected. Surprisingly even the dogs remained silent as we crept into the village looking for the men who had tried to ambush us a few days before.

I had hoped to catch some of them sleeping but we found none of the men we had hoped to find. While we occupied the village, We did find two older men and decided to bring them in for interrogation but as the sun came up over the world, we realized in the light of day they were too old to be combatants and we let them go.

While in a hooch that night I had to hold my pistol to the head of a baby being held by its mother. We thought we heard some male voices outside in the village and I did not want the baby to cry. I told the mother as I pointed the pistol at the baby, in my poor Vietnamese, that she had to keep the baby quiet or I would kill it. The mother was visibly shaking and crying quietly but kept the baby quiet.

When we burst into their hooch's and shined our flashlights in their faces, our automatic weapons pointing at them and faces darkened with camo paint, it absolutely had to scare the hell out of these people. Old people, women, and children were all we found.

I am glad to live in a country like the United States where this sort of thing can't go on and it always seemed awful to me what we had to do in Vietnam. If the folks in the villages would have just cooperated with us and told us what they knew about where the VC were, we wouldn't have been forced to employ those sorts of tactics at all. I felt bad about what we had to do to find intel on the

VC, but it was necessary as the villagers in this area all cooperated with the VC, and it was very likely that the father of the baby was a VC.

The rest of the day after that early morning raid was dull. The remainder of our company was up on top of Hill 55 and I badly wanted to join them for the movie that they were planning on showing that night in the makeshift open-air theater on top of Hill 55. I could not leave my platoon, so I stayed on the bridge and worried about getting overrun due to the terrible condition of the defensive positions we manned.

I spent most nights awake on the bridge after we returned worrying about the men. There was also word going around that we were going to get a new company commander soon. I of course was hoping it would be sooner than later since I had no love for Reneau. That night would further cement my discord with Reneau.

Just before midnight on that evening, we had been experiencing some unusual noise and possibly probing activity outside the wire. I was awake all night until about 2:20 on the morning of August 4th. Ramon, one of my men, threw a grenade at some unidentified noise outside the wire. He was in a particularly tricky defensive position that was on the southeast side of the bridge. The bunker he was in had sunken so much that he had to sit on the roof, a dangerous place from many perspectives, to even get a view out toward the wire. I went across the bridge at that point and talked to him about the grenade and he informed me he had heard some noise and tossed a grenade as precaution. I told him that if he heard more noise, he should toss another grenade and not take any chances.

I went back across the bridge and Ramon threw a second grenade because he heard something. I went back and talked to him about it and he was confident that he heard noises. I told him to continue throwing grenades.

After Ramon threw the first grenade, I got a call on the land line from Reneau and he told me that we were disturbing the people up on Hill 55 and to quit throwing grenades out. He was screaming at me over the land line. I informed him that we were hearing noises and we had to do it. After I came back across the bridge following the second grenade thrown by Ramon, all hell broke loose.

Fucking Sappers! Sappers (a special VC unit used primarily to attack defensive positions) began an incredibly well-planned attack just as I settled back into my bunker. It all started with what had most likely been the source of the noise Ramon heard, the VC laying Bangalore torpedoes in the wire.

189

The torpedoes blew big holes in the wire and allowed the Sappers to begin penetrating our position. They accompanied their assault with a barrage of mortars, rocket fire, rifle grenades, hand grenades and heavy automatic weapons fire. It was a real maelstrom of shooting and they quickly overran two of our positions, killed three of my men and wounded 15 in total.

I ran back and forth across the bridge several times chased by heavy machine gun fire from the southwest corner where the enemy village was located. I must admit that my squad leaders did an outstanding job in getting their squads organized.

There were a lot of individual skirmishes going on inside the wire and I kept communication up with Reneau the best I could. I asked for permission to use the tank we had down on the bridge or even the 106 to ramp things up on our end and maybe put a little fear of God into the Sappers but he shot down the request. Simply saying I was not authorized to fire and I could not do so without his okay. I got the same reply when I requested support from the 81's.

At first, I was completely unaware that the enemy was inside of our wire and I was within about ten feet or so of two of them. It was so damn dark they probably thought I was one of them because they didn't shoot me, and I didn't shoot them either. I thought they were my Marines.

Ramon, unfortunately, was killed that night along with another member of the squad, Belker and Lance Corporal Bobian who survived by playing dead when a VC poked him with an AK47 in the ribs.

At the height of the firefight, we realized all the activity in the wire was a bit of a diversion and that a portion of the team of Sappers had placed two satchel charges (a large number of explosives in a satchel type bag set on a delayed timer) on the bridge in the hope of destroying it all together. I personally found one and tore it down while another one of my Marines found the other one and we both threw them into the river. We had successfully defended the bridge from being damaged but at the high cost of three KIA's and 15 WIA's.

The next day as we surveyed the bridge and inside the perimeter it was littered with evidence of the battle that had taken place just a few hours before. Unexploded grenades and mortar rounds peppered the landscape and shell casings from our .556 M16's and the .762 AK47's were everywhere you walked.

I found it odd that our own battalion commander never came down to view the site, nor did Reneau. I did ,however, receive a visit from the commanding officer of 5th Marines, Colonel Crossfield, and he complimented us on our defense of the bridge against the surprise Sapper attack and subsequently chewed out our CO for not giving us the proper support elements. I was still quite shaken by what had taken place the night before, seeing my own men dead and injured with little I could do to comfort them, and it was extremely gratifying to have at least one senior Marine honor their sacrifice with words of encouragement. It helped me learn that a simple pat on the back at the right time, while it can't bring the dead back, it can build morale, even in the worst situations.

After the attack on the bridge, my platoon was moved back up to Hill 55 on the 7th of August. A day prior to our move an engineer who had been working on the dirt road coming from Hill 55 that went North toward Da Nang and had been wounded by a sniper. So naturally, no rest for the weary, I led a patrol out to the Northeast side of the hill in an area I had not previously been to before.

The object of our patrol of course was to find the sniper and kill or capture him. As we were working our way down toward the river, one of my machine gunners, a big guy, stepped on a 60mm mortar round that had been buried as a booby trap and suffered a terrible wound to one leg and a minor wound to the other.

I again played the role of Corpsman and put a compress on his badly wounded leg, his blood gushed over me. The chunk of his leg missing was so big my hand nearly went through his leg entirely as I applied pressure. I was told later that he would be able to keep his leg but at the time it did not look to me that he would. He was a large man and we had to muscle him up a steep hill in a poncho to a road so he could be medevac'd out of the area. All the way up the hill all he could talk about was that he was going home, he was high on morphine by then, and of course all the other Marines were verbally abusing him for being the biggest man in the squad and making them carry his big ass up the hill. It was all just good-natured ribbing and typical of how Marines dealt with the horrors of war.

Needless to say, the patrol ended there, and we did not find the sniper. When we finally got back to Hill 55 that day however, we found the rest of the battalion had already moved up to Hill 10 and that our company was the only infantry company left on Hill

55. It was an eerie feeling knowing that we were all that stood between the VC and Hill 55 after recent events. I felt almost as if we had targets on our backs, but it was our job to protect regimental headquarters and that was the job we would do.

The good news about being on Hill 55 was that there was a field mess hall and to boot we were also able to get cold beer and I could watch a movie at night if we weren't out on an ambush. Simple pleasures like that kept us all going, I think.

CHAPTER 15
A New Platoon
& A New C.O.

The night of the Sappers attack on Hill 55, our radio went down due to a fragment of shrapnel from a grenade. But not before I told Reneau that he didn't know what he was doing, live over the radio. (Radio which meant everyone could hear). He told me that I was relieved that night,   during the firefight, and I told him to get his ass down to the bridge and relieve me otherwise I was staying in command.

Reneau had lost his mind. The pressure had gotten to him and coupled with his immaturity and lack of military training; he had hurt our company. He was the epitome of what a company commander should not have been. He berated those under him, often he would do so in public, in front of the troops he would call us obscene names, and he consistently made stupid decisions. It wasn't typical of a former enlisted man to be that bad of an officer, but I would later learn he was made to repeat OCS since he was last in his class. In my opinion, he was an embarrassment to the Marine Corps. The good news was that he would be gone in ten days, and I was counting down each one with a smile. The future of our company was to be much better without him in the mix.

Shortly after our battle on Hill 55 against the Sapper attack, I am positive that he thought of it as a punishment Reneau moved me from second platoon to first platoon.

The first platoon commander Lt. Dave Harris had moved on to battalion, and I took over his platoon. Harris left me with an outstanding and well-disciplined platoon. They were a group of hard chargers, and although I did not want to leave second platoon, I welcomed the challenge as a leader. I was lucky to have the support of a fantastic platoon Sergeant named Del Downing as well as an excellent platoon guide Sergeant Joe Lambert and reliable squad leaders, to help me with the transition.

It wasn't uncommon for us to throw 50-100 grenades a night into the river from the

197

bridge on Hill 55. We did this to keep the VC frogmen at bay because they had blown bridges in the area using the method before. I can remember one night standing on the bridge talking to another Marine and I noticed he was nervously looking down at my hand. It had become second nature it seemed for me to have a grenade in my hand and this one already had the pin pulled. I casually tossed the grenade into the river and continued my conversation as the look on his face turned from concern to relief.

August 17th was a fantastic day for Delta Company. That's the day we got our new commanding officer Captain Myers and that dipshit Reneau left Captain Meyers was a good leader and a fine man; he did not have the emotional instability of Lt. Reneau. He would listen to you, take your advice into consideration, and did not swear at or belittle us like Lt. Reneau did. In my opinion, it was a huge mistake to ever put Reneau in command of a rifle company. Captain Meyers had a solid history of being on a Marine sharpshooting team and was a wonderful guy to deal with.

On August 20th, I was back on Hill 55 with my new platoon. Being again at the scene of the previous big fight we went through with a new platoon was a little hairy for me. I didn't really know the men yet, and we had lost so many that night it was hard not to let those thoughts creep into my head.

There had been a lot of improvement on the bridge since I had last been there, thank goodness. The bunkers were reinforced, and the grass finally cleared from the wire, as I had requested long before. But even with the improvement, it was commonplace to find Marines asleep on duty. I felt it was my obligation to be always supervising them because I knew they were all bone tired. As a matter of reality, we could not court martial every Marine that fell asleep or otherwise, we wouldn't have had enough men to take the field. However, we did discipline them, and repeat offenders were subject to office hours.

Each night I would double check to make sure that our claymore mines were placed out properly. If they were placed out in reverse, it would kill our Marines rather than the enemy, and you had to be diligent about placing them, especially with tired Marines doing the placement. We also had to take into consideration the placement of our LP's (listening posts) and had to keep our ambush patrols in the loop as well.

We had intel that the VC were trying to utilize frogmen to take out targets in our area, so I was continually throwing grenades into the river in case the VC came down that way. It wasn't uncommon for us to throw 50-100 grenades a night into the river from the bridge on Hill 55. I can remember one night a patrol from another company had to come back across the bridge to reach Hill 55. I was standing on the bridge talking to the leader of the patrol and I noticed he was nervously looking down at my hand. It had become second nature it seemed for me to have a grenade in my hand and this one already had the pin pulled. I casually tossed the grenade into the river and continued my conversation as the look on his face turned from concern to relief.

We also frequently sent up pop up flares to light up the area, which allowed us to look around with greater fields of view at night.

But you had to be careful, the light from the burning flare attached to a small parachute would play tricks on you as it floated down and drifted with the wind.

There was also a constant radio watch, and I would take turns with my radio operator so neither of us would get too worn out. It was a dangerous job working the radio, it was always the first target for the VC. We would take at least one or two incoming rounds each night from them, just to keep us on our toes, I'm sure.

The next few days were a series of horrific events, the kind of things that make it hard to sleep after you get home. We went out on patrol again and Cpl. Debban, our machine gunner, was shot by a sniper through both legs. We laid down a base of fire but could not get the sniper who shot him. Debban was in a lot of pain until the morphine kicked in. We were unable to get a medevac in to lift him out, and all we could do was sit and watch him die right there in the muddy jungles of Vietnam.

Fresh from watching one of my men die up close I witnessed something even more horrific, something I can still see in my mind's eye to this very day. Captain Jack Perkins (our XO) and I were coming out of the chow hall on Hill 55 when a jeep came speeding in through the wire on Hill 55 just a bit up the road. It was daylight still, and the gates were not put up until nightfall. There were two dead Marines in the back of the jeep, both shot through the head, a wounded Marine in the shotgun seat in the front of the jeep, and the driver of the jeep who was not wounded at all but covered in their blood.

We helped get them out of the jeep and the Corpsmen took care of them, but it was unnerving to see Marines shot so close to our perimeter in broad daylight. Evidently ambushed as they were coming up the finger from the Da Nang side of Hill 55. It was utterly surreal and forever disturbing to my soul.

It wasn't always blood and hell in Vietnam. I finally started receiving a lot of mail and packages from back home. My mother had the good habit of sending me cookies, candy, and Irish whiskey in baby-sized plastic bottles. A girl I had been dating a bit before I left California sent me twelve dozen oatmeal cookies, which by the time they arrived were pretty much oatmeal crumbles. I split them amongst the officers, and we ate them all in style using spoons. I was starting to get a little homesick around this time.

Undoubtedly because I was thinking a lot about my sister, who was getting married on August 20th. I knew it would be a good time since she was marrying a fraternity brother of mine, Joe Abdelnour, and I knew lots of the folks that would be there.

It was a little hard for me to admit at the time, but the truth is around mid-August. I started to suffer from a psychological slump. Maybe it was the thought of my sister getting married, all the cookies from home, or just the fact that we had been getting our asses handed to us recently and not killing any VC in return for our dead. I had lost the zeal I had when I first arrived in Vietnam, but I was determined to get my spirits, and our kill counts back up.

It seemed like all we had been doing lately was taking casualties, and more than anything (yes surprisingly even more than a woman) I wanted to kill Charles (a nickname for the VC). I had dreams of seeing enemy bodies piled high. I knew that it was a morbid and horrifying thought to wish for dead bodies, but when you see so many good friends and young Marines get hit by the enemy, it just becomes routine. It was war after all, and that was the mentality you had to carry with you to survive.

I was determined not to let anything, or anyone get me down. I had made up my mind a long time ago when I decided to join the

Marine Corps that as long as I had a breath of life left in my lungs, I would keep fighting. I came over here to do a job and damn it that's what I intended to do. I even gave myself pep talks to pump myself up each day, but it worked. Sometimes it was hard to see the reasons why we were there, but as a Marine, I wanted to be a good soldier and trust that our country and the world would be better for what we were doing in Vietnam.

I thought about what it might be like to make the ultimate sacrifice of death on the field of battle more times than I probably wanted to admit to myself in those days. I can remember praying that it wouldn't happen and oddly being more concerned with losing a leg than dying. The one thing I was most certain of thought was, that if I did go, I wanted to take some of the enemy out with me.

On the night of August 21st, (my birthday!) I led a patrol out to set up an ambush site near Hill 42 which was west of Hill 55. In the early morning haze on August 22nd, we spotted five VC who were too far away for us to take under fire, but we saw where they had entered a local village. I decided that it would be a good idea to take out another ambush patrol on the night of the 22nd as well, to see if we could get the bad guys coming out of the village the following morning.

Our new Skipper, Captain Myers, gave me permission and I drew up a plan for the patrol and the ambush and that evening took out a 13-man ambush squad. It was a night patrol, and we had to move with exceptional stealth through one village on the way to our target village since the villages all had dogs and lookouts that could give our position away or relay our location and route to the enemy.

When we went on these types of ambushes, we always blackened our faces, although the black Marines would still jokingly complain about having to put the black paint on their faces. I would always insist that they did, however, since I wanted everyone to be treated equally. The black face paint had a mosquito repellant in it, and I wanted to make sure they at least had some of that repellant on them.

We did have plenty of mosquito repellant handy, but the blackface was exceptionally good at repelling those pesky buggers. It also helped to produce a much quieter patrol formation and ambush since everyone wasn't trying to shoo away mosquitoes all the time. We also tied everything down so no piece of equipment or clothing could make noise, shared canteens so they would not slosh around and left our flak jackets and helmets at the base and wore soft covers instead of helmets which allowed us to move with more ease and less noise and not drawing attention from the VC.

Even though this was a nighttime patrol, we were sweating to beat the band, soaking wet from head to toe. At one point I thought to myself "I wonder if I am gushing sweat from the heat or from the fear of our patrol being discovered"?

As we went through the first village, we heard two voices and almost ran into two VC lookouts. Since I knew exactly where we were going, and our point man did not, I actually took point on this patrol. Something platoon commanders were not supposed to do but undoubtedly helped me gain the respect of my new platoon.

There was a stretch where I had to crawl along on my belly, and I was acutely conscientious about trip wires across the trail that might set off a booby trap and about the possibility of a land mine being planted in our path. If I had not before, that night, I became immensely appreciative of what a point man goes through and how hairy a job it really was. It also gave me new respect of how the jungle trails could be more than a little spooky with the ever-present danger of land mines, booby traps and ambushes just waiting out there in the darkness.

After hours of moving along at a snail's pace, we finally reached our destination, but we still had to go through a gate and into the village to set up in the optimal spot. Except the gate had been blocked off and we could not get into the village. So, we went back along our path about 100 meters and set up our ambush site there. There was really nothing else we could do but hope for the best.

We hunkered down and waited on the enemy, and eventually, we saw four VC start out of the gate, but upon seeing our footprints all over in front of the entrance, they beat a hasty retreat into the village. Considering the non-combatants that would be in the village and factoring in the darkness of night, they were not in what I considered a good shooting range. I ordered the men to hold their fire in the hope that they would wait and come back out after a while. So, we waited, and waited, and waited and they never came back out. We were finally forced to go back with our tails between our legs with no kills and no shots fired at all.

A few days later on August 24th, my platoon was picked to demonstrate our M16's to a group of high-ranking officers and congressmen who were in Vietnam to make an inquiry into the M16 and its effectiveness in combat.

The M16 you see had been receiving a lot of bad press, and it was a real problem for us in the field daily. I actually had my Marines tape a cleaning rod to the barrel of their M16's so when a cartridge would jam, they could slam the cleaning rod down the barrel to clear the weapon and continue to fire. The problems were eventually remedied, but many of them never fully trusted the M16 and would have preferred the old M14 instead. Notably I carried a shotgun more than any other weapon as it never misfired and had a good spread.

In any event, we were instructed that under no circumstances were we to lousy-mouth the M16. I was told that no one could say anything bad about it and I stressed this to my platoon when I briefed them about the inspection. The best news of that day was that we were given new utilities and boots and were allowed to clean up somewhat for the inspection which was to take place on Hill 55.

I had my platoon lined up in formation before our VIP's arrived and was reminded again and again not to have my troops bad mouth the M16. A helicopter landed shortly after that brought several congressmen and Marine Generals. They proceeded to walk down my line of Marines with me, accompanying the lead congressman. The answers from my Marines to all of his questions were textbook perfect equating that there were no problems with the M16.

Until of course, the congressman I was accompanying asked one of my Marines how the M16 he had in his hands shot. The young Marine responded, "I do not know sir." I was astounded since we had been in a firefight only two days before and I had seen him firing his M16 myself. The congressman pursued his line of questioning by asking the Marine why he didn't know how his M16 shot. The Marine (whose name I believe was Flores) responded: "Sir, this is not my M16. This M16 belongs to Sanchez. Sanchez is on R&R, and I borrowed his M16 since mine doesn't work worth a shit"

I almost passed out right there on the spot. I got a dirty look from one of the General's and figured my career as a platoon commander was pretty much over at that point. Oddly, the congressmen and senior General's left and nothing else was ever said to me about what had occurred that day. I waited for some form of retribution to come, but none ever did, thankfully.

CHAPTER 16
The Tomato Can & The Purple Heart

If I have failed to mention it yet Vietnam was hot, I mean crazy hot, most of the time. The tents we had were made of such thick canvas that it was always warmer inside than out and sweat was our cologne. We would sweat so much in the heat that we always had to take salt pills and drink water. The water, however, was never right, we still had to put purification tablets into it, which made it taste awful. I was continually reminding my troops to drink water, and in turn, they showed me how Kool-Aid could make it a little more pleasant to drink. We got a lot of Kool-Aid in our care packages from home.

The night of August 28th, I took out a small ambush patrol in an attempt to catch five VC that had been giving us some trouble. They had ambushed at least two of our patrols and wounded a Corpsman and a Machine gunner.

I shouldn't have been taking out such small ambush patrols at night, but I think if we just sat here, we would have all gone nuts. Besides, I really wanted to kill those dudes for what they have done to my unit. I must admit it was a little hairy going out at night. Thank God for our new Skipper, he really understood how this war should be fought and at least let us go out on patrol without flak jackets and helmets on.

The field grade officers seemed to all insist that we wear them each time we go out, but we all hated them. They are a throwback to medieval times, too heavy and too cumbersome to wear in this type of war. They seemed to think we were still fighting the Goddamn Korean war. The truth is you just can't chase down Cong loaded down with heavy gear, and the noise that the equipment creates is a dead giveaway at night when the jungle is quiet.

I have to admit, I tended to get a little concerned when I got some rack time before a night patrol, but the fear would dissipate as

I geared up to go out and walk the jungle with my men. I got excited as we would move slowly through the darkness of night. I usually placed myself two or three spots back from the point man to better control the patrol and keep an eye on my men. It seemed that every day was filled with tension and we were always on full alert like if I let myself relax, it will be the last time ever.

CH-46's began flying over more often around this time taking supplies to regiment. Two of our companies were out on an operation, so it wasn't surprising to me. I was glad to see the support since we were heading out on an operation by Hill 42 the next day. I just wished the VC would have stopped firing at the bridge every night. It seemed to always happen in the middle of the movie the tankers would show across the way. But at least the new Skipper let us have a few beers at night. He played guitar so we would drink, sing songs, and tell jokes while we waited around for Charles to hit us or go on patrol. He was doing his best to help us escape from the harsh realities of Vietnam.

August 30th, we went out on a company operation and to say it was an exciting day would be the understatement of a lifetime. It would turn out to be a bloody day not just for my men but for myself as well.

We were winding up our sweep of the area when I called a squad leaders meeting. We were about to join up with Lieutenant Perkins and Gannon. We were in the village and the squad leaders meeting was just ending when my point man Swan stepped on a tomato can mine, causing it to air burst and wounding eight men including myself.

I was standing next to my radioman talking on the radio when the blast hit me and knocked me down. I was stunned but remember thinking it was a premature explosion from a cave complex we had found that the engineers were getting ready to blow. But when I stood up and saw blood flowing from my hand and my men scattered about in pain on the deck, I knew there was real trouble. I completed my radio traffic with Perkins and assayed the situation. Rainwater was sitting up, holding his knee. with blood gushing out, and I asked how he was, and he said "Sir, this is my third "purp", and I'll be going home!

Swan was hit badly in the head and arms. His helmet, without question, saved his life as it had multiple holes in its shell. Siegel had an incredibly lousy leg wound. So bad in fact that it broke his leg. There were several other wounded with much more manageable injuries like my hand as well. We called right away for an emergency medevac which after what seemed like an eternity showed up and took us out. When Perkins arrived, he ordered me in the medevac. I initially refused, saying my wound was minor, but he firmly ordered me to get in the medevac. We stopped at the 2/5 aid station on the way back and wouldn't you know it, old Lou was standing in the LZ. Joyous to still be alive I jumped off the 46 and gave him a big bear hug. It was nice to see his face, but I hated that I only saw him on the bad days.

After a quick stop and drop at the aid station, they flew us to 1st Med, right near 1st Division HQ. They treated the seriously wounded first and then tended to the shrapnel in me and Cpl. Rainwater. They decided to leave some of the shrapnel in my hand at the time since their facilities were limited and not set up for intricate work like that in the field. The doctor said they would have to cut out too much tissue to get all the pieces out and I might lose the use of my hand. All I could think was that it would be interesting to see how the shrapnel pieces would affect the future use of my hand.

I did, however, get to spend five very relaxing days at 1st Medical Battalion with a real mattress that actually had springs in it, a television in each ward, and nobody shooting at me in the middle of the night. To me, it was R&R.

I got tight with the doctors, and they let me go out to the O club at 1st Med or the Stone Elephant in Da Nang at night since their primary concern was just monitoring me for infection. The wound itself didn't bother me too much, and I drank every night I was there, which I found out was quite the achievement for a WIA. The only big issue for me was that I had to drink with my left hand.

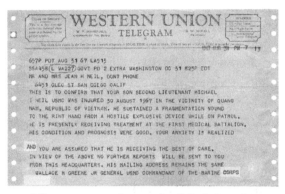

My next morning at 1st Med, I woke up
to the smiling face of Wes Davis, the brother
of one of my fraternity brothers. I had a hard
time believing it at first, it was so
unexpected. He had flown up from Saigon
when he heard I was wounded and stopped
by the hospital to check up on me. So of
course, I finagled permission to leave for the
day, and we went to the Air Force Club at the
Da Nang Air Force Base and got good and
drunk. That's when the real fun started.

We snuck out into Da Nang, which was
off limits that day because it was election day
for the local government. We did some
sneaking around and found the OK Hotel
where we continued to drink and chat up
some local girls. Then headed back to the O

218

club and drank some more before taking in that evening's flick.

On September 4th, I was discharged from the hospital, and Wes came out to the company area with me and spent the night. It was my platoon's turn to take over duties on the bridge that day. I was a little gun shy when we went back to the bridge, which I dreaded at first and was quite the experience for Wes. But him being there and being able to talk to him about what had happened and how it was affecting me now helped me a lot, and after a few hours on the bridge, I felt like my old self again.

Wes, on the other hand, wasn't used to this much action and even though we didn't get hit the night that he was there he jumped at every grenade we threw into the river and every M79 round that was fired. It was understandable though, and I thought it took guts for him to even come down here for the night, not sure I would have in his situation.

I put Wes on a jeep the next day back to Da Nang, and he flew back to Saigon. I can say one thing that those few days in the hospital really impressed upon me was how badly I wanted to go home alive. I had forgotten how good life could be with just a few essential luxuries. I really wanted to see my friends and family again and do all the simple things I loved to do back home. The world to me was still beautiful despite what was going on around me in Vietnam, and I, for sure, wanted to live more life and see more of this fantastic world. But the truth was I could not worry about staying alive, or I wouldn't do a good job, and my men would suffer for that fact. You have to give it 100 percent in battle or else you let your men down. If I were going to catch it, that would be the breaks. I just hoped and prayed I wouldn't catch the big one.

I would receive a Purple Heart for what happened that day as would several of my men, but I think I can say with absolute certainty that no marine or soldier ever awarded a purple heart actually wanted one. We would all much instead have gone our way through the war unscathed. And though I am grateful for the recognition from the Marine Corps and my country for my injuries

I would much rather not have the shrapnel in my hand.

CHAPTER 17
So long Hill 55
Hello Hill 10

One of the worst things about Vietnam; it always seemed to me was the minute you got used to an area, and how to properly defend it from the VC they would up and move you somewhere else.

We got word on September 7th from a Lieutenant in Kilo 3/7 that we would be moving from Hill 55 on September 8th and all I could do was feel sorry for the company moving in, knowing they would take beaucoup casualties on the bridge in our area and the bridge by repeating the same mistakes we made getting to know the area. To try and help them as much as possible I wrote a long and detailed report hoping that the officers who read it would take it to heart and utilize the knowledge, we gained in the lives we lost.

The night before we moved out, I tape recorded a firefight at the bridge and sent it to

Lou. It actually turned out pretty good. We also had a round come through our bunker that night, too close for comfort if you ask me. Luckily, we weren't inside at the time, but you could hear it ricochet around inside, I'm sure if someone were in there, they would have been severely injured at the very least.

Trucks came to pick us up on the bridge that morning, and we then stopped upon Hill 55 to grab the rest of our gear before rolling out to our new home on Hill 10. We drove past a bridge on the way to Da Nang that Charles had blown up a few weeks before. Yet another grim reminder of where we were and why we were there, but it did make me feel a little better about getting off that damn bridge.

When we got to Hill 10, the CO and XO set up in an old French bunker, and I moved my stuff into the staff tent. We had a refrigerator, which we promptly filled with cold beer, electric lights and even a fan in the bunker. They were living the life of Riley on Hill 10, and I was thankful for the upgrade.

I led a patrol out and around our area on our first full day on Hill 10, kind of a get to know your area patrol. I drank quite a bit of beer the night before, and I was hurting a little...okay, I was hurting a lot. I had to keep calling Doc Stull, our Corpsman, up to feed me an aspirin and take the edge off the hangover. Man, what a head I had. The patrol was uneventful, and a pleasant sojourn into our new area which didn't seem like it would be too problematic at the time, except for the expected landmines and booby traps which were still high on everyone's list of concerns.

We had an excellent little song fest over at the Top's (Marine for 1st Sergeant) hooch on September 10th. He and this other Top both played guitars, and it was easy for us all to get lost in some songs and drink some beers for a while. At that time, I remember feeling like I just had to get out of there for some R&R or just going on a float would be good enough for a recharge. The thought of it was keeping me going at the time. Oh, how I wanted to see a woman, drink in a comfortable place, and just relax, or raise hell, without having to be responsible for anyone else and without getting shot at all the time.

On September 14th we had a battalion change of command ceremony. My platoon was one of the two at the ceremony. What a joke it was, so much dog and pony, they actually made us wear leather boots, regular utilities with the new camouflage covers. We really should have been able to just wear what we wore in the field.

We had quite the party the night of the 13th in the Tops hooch celebrating Harris making 1st Lieutenant. I firemen-carried him home, and he ended up puking all over me, which caused me to fall down with him launching me into some barbed wire and ripping the brand-new rain jacket the folks sent me from home. That entire debacle made it a little difficult to stand at attention in the heat during the change of command ceremony on the 14th but they had free beer afterward, and a little hair of the dog and the opportunity to drink a few with some of the troops for a while made everything come back into focus. I can honestly say they were some magnificent men, and if the world at that time had been filled with more men like them, it would be a better place today. Tom

Brokaw called WWII veterans the greatest generation. It has been suggested that Vietnam veterans be called the "finest Generation" and I would agree.

Golf Battery Artillery was with us on Hill 10, and the 105 rounds would sometimes scare the hell out of us. I would honestly jump sometimes when they fired. It seemed worse after the incident with the tomato can, I wouldn't realize how much loud noises really got to me until some years later back in my real world outside of the war in Vietnam. At the time we would fight it off with jokes, and it helped to work out if we could take our minds out of the war, but some days it was hard to force yourself to work out. I did try to do it regularly and probably would have done it more if I could shower afterward. Oh well, war is hell.

Judy wrote, and she said she wanted to meet me on R and R and that she had a patron at her clothing store who would pay her way. Still not really sure what that was all about. But I remember thinking it would be good to see her as long as she had no serious designs on a future together because I sure didn't have any. I liked her, don't get me wrong, she was a good woman, but I knew marriage would never happen with her.

Anyway, I figured if we got to go to Okinawa on a pass, I wouldn't even bother with R&R because Oki would have been good enough. I could already feel the

227

massages and the steam baths were a must. I had a grand plan to get three of them right off the bat before I did anything else, as I wanted to make sure I had washed Vietnam entirely out. Blood is harder to wash off than dirt, especially the blood of your close friends, and you will find a few more intimate friends than those you make in combat.

The hardest and most dangerous part of moving into a new area in Vietnam was figuring out the area and where to take patrols. We wanted to find Charles and kill him not walk around in the jungle for no reason sweating our balls off.

Hill 10 had a small and ill-defined patrol area, and we ran so many patrols that we would often run into each other. It was dangerous, and I was afraid that at some point, we might end up shooting our own men or vice versa.

September 16th, I took out a three-day patrol into the mouth of Happy Valley. It was an NVA infiltration route for men and more importantly rockets. If we could capture or destroy rockets it was a big win for us. It was a reasonably exciting patrol but quite a miserable one since the monsoon season had just started. We couldn't tell at that point if we were soaked in rain or sweat from the heat.

The first night out we broke into three squad sized ambushes, and I actually thought we had something on the way out, but it was most likely one of our own patrols. The rest of the night was a miserable time fending off gnats and mosquitoes, they almost ate me alive despite the repellant. The worst part about the insects is the mental torture those little buggers inflict on you. You can't slap at them to kill them because you give away your position and you can't focus on them either because you might miss Charles walking up on you. Just one more fun part of this lovely war.

The next two nights, I sat up on the ridgeline that overlooked two valley floors. It was a fantastic OP (Observation Post) with clear sight lines of the valley. I could see so well that I called in my first arty (Artillery) strike on eight dudes we saw humping through the valley. We must have gotten at least one of them, when the rounds dropped on them, they scattered like roaches but not soon enough.

We got back on September 19th and had a little get together to celebrate. The next day we moved down to Tuy Loan Bridge and wouldn't you know it there was GTO. He was a great little Viet kid and often helped to act as our interpreter and could really clean an M16. He also serves as our chief ass kicker for the local kids. They were always around and could be quite the nuisance. Don't get me wrong, they were good kids and didn't steal anything or cause trouble, but the brass didn't want them around, so we were continually showing them away, and we let GTO hang around because he helped us out.

At least the men got a break down on the bridge. We only had to run one short patrol each day, but I still hated the responsibility for bridges. They were never adequately fortified, and you were always just sitting out there in the open waiting for a sniper to pick you off or a rocket to come flying in and blow you to pieces. It really added to the tension of an already tense place.

We did get an excellent opportunity to fortify our positions by laying wire, filling, and clearing our fields of fire. I always tried

231

to keep myself and the men busy, it helped keep away the depression of war that would find its way into all our heads eventually.

On September 24th I got to go into Da Nang with our guide Cpl. Healey and GTO. It was just what I needed for a bit of recharge. Spent a lot of time at the PX (Post Exchange) and picked up some hot peppers and steak sauce to jazz up the C-rats (technically they were MCI – Meal Combat Individual rations, but we all called them C-rats) which helps, they aren't really that good.

GTO had a great time in Da Nang that day just sitting out in the beer garden with us as we downed a few brews. The Marines and Viet women working there were fascinated with him, and all stopped by to give him a look. Probably because we had him dressed up as a junior Marine and he played the role so well. But eventually, duty called, as it always does, and the fun had to end. So, we headed back to the Bridge a short while later.

Shortly after we got back, one of my men shot a dog inside our wire. Battalion had us on 100 percent alert for five straight nights and tensions were high. My adrenalin was really pumping as I heard a noise and thought we really had some action. I grabbed my .45 and a couple of grenades and ran out to investigate, but it was only a local dog. Bridge security really made us all jumpy, and we never got any sleep at night. At least out in the field, you have the freedom of movement and some mobility. Just sitting around and waiting for something to happen was not my kind of war.

I could not imagine what it was going to be like to someday be able to finally relax again. The responsibility in Vietnam was good for me, and I felt as if I was finally gaining some of the maturity I lacked, but it was a hard way to learn, a real-life trial by fire situation if you will.

What I really wanted to do was hold a woman in my arms again and be alone someplace where I had no cares or worries, and the rest of the world be damned. I wanted to sip cold drinks by the ocean and feel that relaxing calm wash over me. I wanted to play sports again, to run and swim, to be turned on my life again. The world I was living in was like a deadly Keystone comedy.

Things in that time in that world were already bad enough, but that night the generator for the lights on the river broke down, the rope on the gate in the river broke, and our motorboat wouldn't run. There were always issues, but now it would be easy for a Frogman to blow the bridge and then someone would blame my sorry ass because as always, shit rolls downhill. So, I just figured they could go fuck themselves and the horse they rode in on.

We all were doing what we could with the tools we had and if the Marine Corps had to have a scapegoat for whatever happened and it happened to be me it would have forever shattered my faith in the Marine Corps, and I would have just told them to shove the whole mess where the sun doesn't shine. I figured I was a lawyer and I had my own world to return too.

I had no idea at the time I would turn out to be a career Marine much less end up as a Brigadier General. So, the thought of being fearful of every move I made so I wouldn't end up with a bad fitness report never really crossed my mind. Too many officers were also concerned with their own petty careers in Vietnam instead of winning the war. They just wanted to please their superiors, not kill Cong and delight the locals.

That issue of pettiness coupled with the outdated Korean War tactics that many of the senior officers employed at the time often made proper conduct in that war a problematic task. But I gave it everything I had and luckily it was enough, I knew I would at least have the satisfaction of knowing I was the kind of man who had the guts to do the right thing and didn't shirk from my duty as I saw it. My thought was if nothing else I would be true to myself. Hell, it was probably that very attitude that took me so far, and I can tell you I always appreciated it when I saw the same kind of moxie in a young officer under my command.

Finally, after a very long wait and several letters of my own, I got a letter from Donna. I bet I read that letter ten times the first day alone. She sure was a good-looking girl, appeared to be lovely in my eyes and boy oh boy what a figure she had on her. I will definitely look her up when I get home. I wrote her an eleven-page letter the same night.

I also got a letter from Kay that day, she said it was hard for her to write to me knowing where I was and why I was there. It was good to hear from her (from anyone really), and she certainly was good to me, too bad I could never have loved her.

I often wondered if that was just the way it was, the person who you would probably be best mated with in life was one you could never love? But I still wanted to see her when I got home too, along with Donna and any other good-looking gal that I could see.

Man, I really, I mean really, missed women! All that no women jazz was for the birds if you asked me. I planned to make up for lost time from my prison of forced celibacy on my return to the real world.

The bad news that day was that one of my men, named Chapman from my unit who was wounded while I was in the hospital recovering from my hand wound, died yesterday in the hospital. He was a good

Marine and a hell of an M79 gunner and was missed in many battles to come.

On Sep 27 I went back to 2nd platoon for 2 nights while Lt. Harris went on R and R. I remember the second night vividly as we had set up in a VC village which was actually a complex of three separate hooches, and 2nd platoon had killed a VC in this complex 4 nights before and we hoped to catch at least 1 VC coming back to visit. We moved 14 women and children into 1 of the hooches while we waited in ambush. two of the children were crying too much and that concerned us and we made the women quiet them down . I fell asleep on one of their bamboo racks and I was awakened by a little puppy who was so hungry I also remember a little girl from that night who had gold earrings and a gold ankle bracelet but was filthy dirty.

I always felt sorry for the villagers when we had to put them in those types of situations. The little girl with big dark eyes and a gold ankle bracelet really stood out to me on this ambush. She seemed so hopeful, but sadness filled her eyes. I could never seem to fully grasp why the villagers never seemed to wash their dishes, clothes, or themselves for that matter. They sure had access to plenty of water, but they just seemed to neglect their hygiene, it really made me feel sorry for the kids more than anything.

I always felt sorry for the animals in the villages too. The Vietnamese don't seem to have the same affection for animals as Americans do, they treat their animals as more a functional part of the community serving as alarm systems and pest control more than pets. You should have seen this little puppy in the village that day, he was so savage when I gave him some rice this morning, I thought he was going to eat my hand along with the rice. After we came in from the ambush, I had a meeting with Lieutenant Colonel Davis in preparation for a meeting with General Masters and Colonel Dohler from The Basic School. I looked forward to seeing them again. They were there to talk to Pinckert and me as recent graduates of The Basic School so we could give them feedback on our training and how it applied to our time in Vietnam.

Had a few beers and a good cigar with Jack that night and talked about the months to come. He, much like myself, was getting bored with our current posting. It was just so routine and dull we wanted to do something else, anything else. So, I asked him why he didn't put in for a transfer. I knew that if we didn't go on a float (Marine for being on a ship), I was going to put in for a transfer to Recon (Marine for Reconnaissance Operations)

I also got another package from Judy that day more homemade cookies and a pint of Canadian Club. She sure knows what a man needs. I must have eaten 30 cookies. Too bad she wasn't younger; she was a real good woman, and I am planning on hooking up with her in Hawaii on R&R if it works out.

October 1st was a relatively uneventful day, which in a war zone is a good thing. Sergeant Downing had a cup of coffee waiting for me that morning when I got up, and I had a pleasant stroll down to the river enjoying it. I had to wait a bit on a couple of young girls who were there washing their hair before I washed and shaved. I will say this for the Vietnamese women, for the most part, they have coal black hair that is very pretty.

Top and Jack Perkins came by and paid the platoon, and I gave them a shot of the Canadian Club Judy sent. I then gave a lecture to the men on patrolling and ambush techniques, and Sergeant Downing gave a follow-up lecture on mines and booby trap signs. We were continually losing and getting new troops, so we had to keep them up to speed. We had a quick rifle inspection before chow, which was steak that night, a sweet treat. Then followed it up with some beers with Corporal Healey, Sgt. Lambert and Sgt. Downing to cap off the day. We had a good talk about the Marine Corps, women, Santo Domingo, and WWII. Like I said before, the days were getting routine and we were all getting bored. But I will say it again. War is 99.9 percent boredom and .01 percent, sheer terror.

The night prior one of our LP's spotted five VC, took some shots at them and high tailed it back into the wire. I fired some 106 rounds as well as some 60mm rounds at them and then sent a squad out to check the area. I subsequently got my ass chewed out over the radio by battalion for letting my people put rounds down range without being able to positively identify someone as VC in pitch darkness. Which was total bullshit because the locals knew better than to come within 50 meters of the wire at night so it could have only been VC. I always operated with that in mind, and if they came within 50 meters of our wire, they were going to get blown away and to hell with the battalion.

241

GTO was there every day and had really become a good sidekick. Today he said the funniest thing: "Navy is number 10,000, Marine Corps is number fucking 10,000,000, Civilian is number one" Amen to that thought.

CHAPTER 18
So Long Hill 10
Hello, Hill 41

Another day on the bridge on Hill 10, by this time the days were just rolling into one another. On October 5th my platoon moved to Hill 41 to man the Bravo company lines for six-days while they were out on an operation, but I stayed behind with second platoon until Lieutenant Harris got back on October 6th. Second platoon was mostly new men at this point, they had a very competent platoon sergeant named Burns, but he was new to the Nam and even though he was learning fast, the battalion thought it best I stay with second until Harris returned.

Doc Lucas noted that the latrine on the bridge was filling up. One day he decided to change the location, which he did. He had a couple of marines dig a new hole on the same side, adjacent... He had the men fill in the old one. The monsoon had started and it rained all night. Nobody told Kuykendall, who was on patrol, when he returned late in the day, and needed to take a crap and raced for the shitter . He fell in, up to his armpits. Tallest man...Gonna kill you, Doc Lucas. Found a rope and pulled him, chased Doc L around, Lucas everyone laughing. told him to throw himself and his clothing into the river.   Sometimes you would hear random shouts of "Who Dat" coming from all around in yet another attempt to bring a little levity to our lives and keep the war off our minds. We had nicknamed one of our fellow Marines named Hudak "Who Dat" and every time you heard someone shout it you laughed just a little bit. But that's how it was with pretty much everything. You did what you could to minimize the mental effect the war had on you. Our hooch was like most in war, an eclectic mix of all the personalities living in the space. The radio was in the corner, and I made sure the C-rats were always stacked high in front of it to block the light so I could sleep. There was a large American flag on the far-right side of the tent that the locals made for us. It only had one side and was facing the wrong way, but we hung it up anyway as it was a nice gesture and helped with local relations.

  That night we were on 100 percent alert

again, but the first game of the world series between the Boston Red Sox and Saint Louis Cardinals playing over the radio was the only noise. Except for the snoring of Corporal Healey who fell asleep with his face on the radio. War makes you tired as a dog, and Marines can fall asleep anytime anywhere if they know someone has their back. I had stopped eating any real breakfast around this time and would often just have a few cups of coffee and some raisins in its place as I felt two meals a day was enough. The C-rats were high calorie, and we weren't really doing a lot of patrolling. I started doing pull-ups, sit-ups, pushups, and running about ten minutes a day just to keep in shape on days that we didn't patrol at all. Running was just too great for words to me, and it really made me feel great, helped to relieve tension, relaxed me, and kept me fit. I knew that if I were able after the war, I would keep running for the rest of my life as an emotional and mental outlet that had the bonus of keeping me fit and trim. I figured I would stay with the company for maybe two more months to see if they went on a float, I'll believe the rumor when I see it through. I talked to Captain Rupp from force recon on October 4th when they came to inspect the bridge. He

245

told me to put in an AA form, and I could definitely get a recon spot. I really needed a change, more mental than physical since this was not my idea of how to fight a war.

Sitting on a bridge with an inadequate defense was not my idea of being a Marine. I wanted to kill Cong and was utterly fed up with the line company bullshit of worrying about policing the area, shining my boots and pleasing my superior officers instead of fighting the war.

We were fighting the war wrong in my opinion, as I saw it, we had two courses of action. We could place all the Viet people in protected, secured areas where we can keep Charlie away from them day and night. Which would effectively cut him off from the people and hurt him where it hurts most, revenue and supply line. Charlie lived off the local people to survive, so we had to cut off that link somehow. Even the locals who didn't want to cooperate with Charlie had to, or they would just be killed. I really felt sorry for them being caught in the middle of the war. They really only cooperated with Charles because we were more forgiving.

They actually preferred us over Charlie because we didn't take half of their crops like Charlie did nor did we conscript their young men for a lifetime of military service to fight for a cause they don't really believe in at all.

Our second option would have been to completely destroy and lay waste to anything that offers us resistance, just like the South Koreans did there. So, if we received any fire from a village or uncovered trip mines or booby traps or found evidence of VC sympathy, we would destroy the village and kill every living thing in the village as well. This, of course, would have been a brutal approach but would have kept within the realities of the war.

The wishy-washy way we were fighting the war was only getting us more dead Marines. We needed to take a firm approach and stop trying to be the friendly people holding "county fairs" and leaving. We sat up on our nicely defined hills in a defensive posture and expected that we would win the war. The Viet people were the key to winning the war, so the only way to win was to keep Charlie away by either giving them adequate protection or destroying them if they helped Charles. For the record, I was a proponent of protection, but if I am honest, I had my days when I just wanted to lay waste to the land.

I always had glimpses of sunshine in Vietnam to take away the darkness of the situation and often, it was GTO that brought the rays. One day I remember going to the Ville (what we called the village) with GTO to have a look around and his father, the village barber, gave me a haircut and a shave.

248

He was an honorable man and even though I insisted he would not let me pay for his services because we helped to protect his village.

It always amazed me how different this village was from the one on Hill 55. The people were industrious, relatively clean, and were very anti-VC. The PF platoon commander gave me a tour of his defenses, and man were they piss-poor. Their bunkers were just a few sandbags at different places around the perimeter and some scroungy wire that looked sorry. I promised them some sandbags and new wire and the PF commander was overjoyed. I just hoped Charles didn't make a determined attack on the Ville because they would have been overrun, no sweat.

I was out on patrol that day with Sergeant Lambert's squad, and we had just crossed highway 5 and entered a Ville when the VC soldier ran out trying to escape. We yelled at him to stop (by this time my Vietnamese was getting pretty good) but still had to fire a warning shot before he stopped running. Sergeant Lambert then went up to question him while I stayed back and covered him. As he approached the man, an obvious fanatic, was cursing him in Vietnamese and threw a ChiCom (hand grenade) at him, prompting Lambert to shoot him. He was still reaching for another grenade when I shot him, emptying my M16 into him. I then ran up to him and started shooting him with my 45, when I heard Sgt Lambert say, "I think he is dead, sir." I got too excited, and wasted ammunition on a dead man

We ended up getting some letters off him and brought in a young girl who was with him in the hooch he ran from. I have to say as much as I regretted that I had to put him down, it felt pretty good to kill that bastard at the time in retribution for all my lost Marines and close friends, but our company still had a long way to go to even that score.

I had a chance to go into Da Nang and met a marine from Marble Mountain, where I hoped to find Sigler.

but he was still up in Dong Ha it seemed. Man did those AO's have it made! Hot water for showers and an excellent O club that was the life. I hitched a ride back via various vehicles and stopped at the bridge and had a beer with Harris.

That night was the night Selkreg was killed by a "friendly" 60mm fragment as they were fan firing 60mm mortars. He had not buttoned up his flak jacket and a fragment of a friendly mortar round skipped across the river into Selkrig's bunker and struck him in the open part where the flak jacket was not buttoned. He was a very popular marine machine gunner and his death stunned us all.

The next morning was a rough one for me. I would learn of the death of my good friend John Norris from Pinckert who told me he had been killed in an ambush over by Hill 55. Apparently, he was shot directly through the heart as he was walking point. Although I had done it myself, I couldn't believe he was walking point. He should have known better damn it! I thought he always did have more guts than brains. In reality, he was very bright.

It was a shame and hit me hard. He was a good man, and I would miss his friendship. Just one more reason to kill Charlie in my mind, though. I took it upon myself to write a letter of condolence to his wife Connie that night, she was a good woman, and I felt for her loss. It seemed ironic then I guess all the jokes we made in The Basic School about how if John ever got it in Vietnam, I would take care of her if I made it home. I planned to honor my word and check on her when I got back if I got back.

We got word on the night of October 14th that we would be moving back to Hill 41 permanently. I remember hoping that for once the word was accurate because I really needed to get away from the petty battalion bullshit and our First Sergeant who was starting to get on everyone's nerves.

Went on patrol that night with Corporal Dohra's squad. Man were the rice paddies high. It must have taken us a half an hour to get through one of them.

It may not have been this day but I clearly remember an incident crossing a rice paddy that I must convey. Trudeau was carrying my radio and was right behind me when someone yelled. He was very short and had stepped into a 155 crater in the rice paddy. I turned around looking for him and all I could see was the tip of the antenna sticking out of the water. I dove in, grabbed him, and sputtering and spitting water he came to the surface. Everyone had a good laugh at his expense.

The mud would just suction your feet when you stepped into it so hard it was like walking in wet cement. Then you would slip and fall on your ass as you tried to keep your balance while you pulled your foot out of the mud trying to stay on the highest part of the paddy dike. Seemed like when we weren't waist deep in water, we were humping up hills. It was not a good patrol by any standard, wet, nasty, sweaty, and no kills.

I went into Da Nang again on the 24th of October to go to a personal response school but ended up not going and just going out and getting loaded with Bob Petrella instead. It was election night again, and we weren't even supposed to be out in the town, but we were looking for that civilian's house and couldn't find it at all. We were so loaded. Until we got stopped by some MP's while we were riding around in a pedicab with some beer in our hands (that was frowned upon by command) and they just ended up taking us there since they knew him.

I went back to Hill 41 the next day and was a little sick but still went out on a reaction force the next day when one of my squads that was out on patrol was surprised by about 30 VC. It was a hell of a night and a hell of a fight. We scraped together the cooks, extra radiomen, supply men and anyone else we could find to make up the reaction force. But by the time we got there, and the battle was over, we didn't find anything worthwhile. Luckily nobody in my squad was hurt in the fire fight, but I was a little pissed at the squad leader for not calling in some ARTY on their position.

The next three days or so I was sick as a dog. Super thirsty and drank as much as I could keep down but couldn't stomach food at all. I had a headache, muscle aches, a slight bladder infection, and was incredibly weak. I bet I slept for at least eighteen hours that day. The battalion Doc (John Hatchett) gave me some pills that seemed to clear it all up, but I was still weak from not eating for three days, I guess. I sure would have liked to know what the hell happened to me, but there aren't any labs in a war zone so if you're not dying you just have to ride it out and make do.

Like I said in the darkness of war, you seem to always find some bright spots to help you muscle through the dark days. Coming off my sickness, I received all kinds of mail from Dick Roppe's 6th-grade class. Some of the letters were funny, the kind you only get from a child's honesty. I wrote them back and thanked them for thinking of us. I also got letters from Connie, Delle and best of all, Donna. Man was that woman a doll! She could write one hell of a sexy letter, and I read them over and over. She mentioned going to the bullfights when I got back, and I almost keeled over laughing. All I could think about was how good it was going to be with a real, delicate, sexy, feminine woman again.

We got some boots (new Marine's) on October 15th, but I lost Sergeant Downing to Bravo company. Sergeant Lambert became my new platoon Sergeant, Corporal Healey was my guide at this point, and Dohra, Campbell and Kurts were my squad leaders. Lambert took out a recon patrol tonight, they looked pretty good in the new camouflaged utilities. I like them better. They help break up your pattern more and make us harder to spot on patrol.

They were gung-ho about it as was the rest of my platoon.

By this time, my R&R was only four days away. I couldn't even imagine what it was going to be like. I was all set to meet Judy, but I gave her pretty short notice, and if she didn't make it, I was still determined to have a ball anyway. My first mission on R&R was going to be to soak out all the dirt with a hot tub and a shower or maybe both. I had only had one shower in the last month, and it was a cold one at that, field showers suck. Next, I planned on putting on some civvies (Marine for civilian clothes) and enjoying the pure luxury of not wearing utilities that smell and are caked with dirt and blood all day. Then the plan was to leap into my rented Mustang and spin-off to the airport, pick up Judy, and

get her back to the hotel as fast as those
wheels would carry me.

CHAPTER 19
R & R

I was scheduled to leave for R&R on November 2nd, so I made sure I went out on patrol the night before, so I could remember just exactly how rotten Vietnam could be when I got there.

I took $400 and went into Da Nang on November 1st, met up with Rocky MacPherson from our battalion and John LeBlond from up north, Drs. Hatchett and Barton and really raised some hell at the Stone Elephant and the MAC V clubs. Tom Keene was with us that night as well, and I left my gear at his MP company. I had planned to spend the night at his MP company.

We finally made it back and I told the night watch to make sure and wake me up no matter what or I would cut off his balls. He listened well and woke me up at 0430 on the nose. I was still incredibly drunk, and it took me fifteen minutes to wake up before I stumbled my way down to the RR center for my flight.

The flight to Hawaii went smooth and it was sure nice to see some round-eyed American stewardesses walking the aisles of the plane. We stopped over in Guam for an hour on the way and I picked up 5 bottles of good liquor for $10.30 (free port prices) and some shaving gear since I left mine at the R&R center in Da Nang. I went to the head and quickly shaved before hopping back on the flight to Hawaii. We landed at 0430 and as I walked off the plane, I can remember it was balmy out and looked like I was walking into heaven.

They put us on a bus and took us out to the R&R center at Fort DeRussy and after a short briefing on the do's and don'ts of R&R in Hawaii and then we were free to go our merry way.

I checked into my hotel, got in a quick workout of push-ups and sit-ups, and took two very long, very hot showers. I put on a clean khaki uniform and went out to breakfast.

Then I rented a Mustang convertible and took a drive up to Punahou, my old school. The school's campus had changed some but looked basically how I remembered it from my school days. It had impressively kept pace with the times and gave me a flush of memories of the past when at 0800 they played the national anthem and all the kids came to attention and sang to old glory. I looked up my former coach Mr. Jim Doole, who remembered me, and he was kind enough to show me around the entire school. I headed over to Pearl Harbor, picked up some civilian clothes from the PX, and tried to look up Sergeant Belinski, my old OCS platoon Sergeant, but had no luck. So, I hopped back into the Mustang and cruised over to the airport to meet up with Judy. I got there with time to spare so I got drunk at the airport bar.

So drunk I missed her getting off the plane but found her outside. We grabbed her luggage and headed directly to the hotel. After a quick beer and mixer run the marathon began and that was pretty much the story for the rest of R&R.

I did get a chance while I was there to hang out with my friend Henry Lee, his wife and his little boy Eleu. We had a blast! Went to his folk's house and had the best rice and teriyaki ever then went to Shipwreck Kelly's with Henry.

I closed out my R&R in Hawaii by spending the last two evenings with John LeBlond and his wife. What a great couple they were, really in love with each other, we had a lot of laughs. The final night I even put a coat and tie on for dinner with them at the O club at Fort Rutger... We finished off the evening at the Don Ho show.

At 0430 the next morning the front desk called, and the beginning of the end arrived with the call. It was time to go back to Vietnam. I kissed Judy goodbye and took a cab to the R&R center where we caught the bus to the airport. I got to make a couple of phone calls while I was there, one to John Low, who really did me a solid favor by sending some of my civilian clothes in the care of Judy. The other, to my family back in the states. I was lucky enough to be able to

talk to everyone for quite a while and it made
my heart feel good to hear their voices.

CHAPTER 20
Meanwhile Back on Hill 41

Two days after I got back from R&R in Hawaii, I went out on a five-man recon patrol over by the river. It was colder than hell that night and rained non-stop. The patrol was uneventful but a good reminder of how crappy a place Vietnam was when all you were there for was war. I already missed the civilian world of luxury

The morning after that five-man recon patrol we killed two VC who were sneaking along the river. I was questioned later by the battalion S-2 (Marine for Intelligence and Security officer) about the shooting. It seemed someone, I suspect it was a village leader, was claiming they were innocent farmers. I however was convinced they were VC. Mostly because this patrol was in the Bo Ban's area and communist sentiment ran high there. It was known as a free fire zone, and we had permission to fire on site at anyone

263

we suspected to be VC. So, it was usually assumed that fighting aged men were VC and that was what this war really was, ugly and difficult to tell the good from the bad.

You had to be wary of everyone and nice to everyone at the same time. I am convinced that had I not been with my men who backed up my actions that day there would have been a big investigation and possibly a court-martial. But since I was an officer with an outstanding record and had the word of my men to back me up, they took my word over the village leaders and smoothed it all over.

November 15th, I took my platoon out along the Bo Ban river as a blocking force and a force from Bravo company swept towards us in the morning. We spotted a VC, shot at him and gave chase. Campbell, my 1st squad leader, tripped a booby trap in the pursuit and suffered multiple wounds to his leg, I can still hear him yelling when I close my eyes to this day. The medevac that came in to get him was the best I had ever seen. We had him all prepped to go when it landed, I grabbed the stretcher and we got him in and off to the aid station in record time. Dohanish did a fine job of calling it in, I found another booby trap close to the explosion that got Campbell and blew it up to make sure it wouldn't do the same to the next man. Scared the ever-loving crap out of me when I moved it, setting the C-4 next to it though, talk about pucker factor. I swore next time I would have a private blow the trap and save me the clinch.

Two days later November 17th I took the platoon out on a two-day patrol. We shot a VC in the brush on the way out when my point man almost stepped on him. We then broke down into three squad size ambushes for the night and rendezvoused the next morning. I got no sleep that night at all, nor did many of my men, since we were soaking wet from the dew in the dense bush and it was also freezing cold. But as luck would have it, I found some holes in my trousers and apparently the mosquitoes discovered them as well and they promptly bit me on my ass and balls. I never said it was good luck.

The next day I led my platoon into Mortar Valley (called so because the VC had a proclivity to launch mortar attacks from that valley) leaving our packs with third squad so we could go in quick and quiet. About an hour out we heard voices ahead of us around 200 meters, so I took five men, and we went to investigate. We crossed over a small steam and before we knew it the voices were all around us. We couldn't advance through the brush because it was too dense, so we beat feet back to the rest of the patrol. Fortunately, I had two ARTY FO's with me, a Lieutenant, Pete Ruane and an enlisted Marine Dutch van Fleet who stayed in the corps ? .... I cancelled the ARTY and instead called in an air strike that was a thing of beauty. I talked to the AO overhead and helped to coordinate a precision drop of napalm by 2 A-4s. We could hear the VC screaming as they were burned alive by the napalm and all of us were screaming and yelling "get some' A piece of shrapnel from one of the napalm bombs landed on my flak jack and burned through it, (we were that close to the airstrike!)We also had our yellow panels out to mark our position. My men were flat on the ground and none of them were hit. This was my first airstrike, and Pete and Dutch were a big help calling it in.

After the air strike we moved in to search the area and Kurtz's squad found a cave complex, that was halfway up the trail to Charlie Ridge. so, we all joined up there. Kurtz shot and wounded an NVA who was trying to run back up the trail and escape in the effort. The caves themselves were well hidden and could only be accessed by walking up a steep trail. We had found a real NVA base camp and quickly nicknamed it the Ho Chi Hilton.

We destroyed over 600 pounds of rice, cooking utensils, sleeping quarters, clothing, M1 rounds, canteens and even two live chickens. Battalion and Captain Meyers were impressed and quite pleased with our find, but I was pissed off that we found no dead bodies after that air support. All we found was blood trails, which was typical, Charles was pretty good at taking their dead and wounded with them. We found a can of Nuoc Mam- a Vietnamese type of sauce, and we poured it into the creek that ran parallel to the trail so they couldn't use it. We had left our packs with third squad and while third squad was waiting for us a bunch of the men dove into the stream to get a drink of water and I heard several of them yelling "Shit! This tastes like Nuoc Mam! I had to laugh at how fast it had travelled from the creek to the stream.

Our radios had actually stopped working. I believed it was caused by the enemy and I sensed that something was wrong and it was only a matter of time before they set up an ambush and hit us as we went down the trail. So I got the platoon together and I led them double timing down the trail without incident.

We split off again and headed out to our ambush sites for the night. The men did such a good job and the night was so quiet (which we expected after blowing up half the valley) that I asked the Skipper if we could cut the patrol short and come in the next day, which he said was okay. For good measure we hit Phuoc Ninh on the way back in with no results. That place was a damn VC Ville if ever there was one.

The night after we came back in was Captain Meyers last night with us so of course, staying true to Marine form, we got some beer and whiskey and had a going away party for him. Sargent Downing and Dave Harris even came over from Hill 10 and spent the night. It was a good time and I would certainly miss Captain Meyers in the days to come. He was a good man and did a lot for our company. He was easy to get along with, understanding and knew his shit that's for sure. I personally learned a lot from him, and I felt that everyone else benefited from his leadership as well. Our new Skipper, Captain Blechfeld, on the other hand was young and a hard charger. He had been a staff officer at division before coming to us, and my biggest hope at this point was that we would just get along well.

I went into Da Nang on Nov 22 with Gy Smith and Perkins who was going on R&R to Japan. We were stopped on the way in because the mine sweeping had not been completed. We were right behind a diesel tanker truck that had a marine riding shotgun with a shotgun across his lap sitting on top of the cab of the tanker. Inside the cabin were the Vietnamese driver and 2 other Vietnamese. Once the all clear sounded and

269

we started driving again on the dirt road when the tanker truck hit a huge landmine. I can remember seeing the Marine flying through the air along with the Vietnamese who had been blown out of the cabin. The explosion was horrific. The three of us jumped out of the jeep and ran to get the bodies and I picked up one of the Vietnamese who felt like a limp rag. Every bone in his body appeared to be broken and he was dead. By the time I got back to the roadway I saw the corpsman start to give first aid to the Marine. He was doing CPR and would breathe, spit out the blood, breathe again, spit again to the side. It was absolutely horrific to watch and that corpsman deserved every accolade he could get. We had to keep on going and I found out later on that every occupant of the truck died. including the Marine which was not a surprise. It was a hell of a way to start a day– but thank God it was not atypical.

It was one of those things that I would add to my list of things I could never be unseen. It was a growing list everyday it seemed. Vietnam was wearing thin on me.

When I got back to our area after dropping off Perkins finally, I led a reactionary force out when one of our patrols spotted 100 VC moving out of Happy Valley. We spent all night and part of the next day searching the area and ended up finding a dead VC with his AK-47 and some gear. We set up an ambush and I think it may have been the spookiest night in the bush yet, I got no sleep at all thinking about the VC out there and that poor mangled Marine from the gas truck explosion.

We busted our asses humping that valley looking for Charles that day and battalion was convinced that we stopped another rocket attack. We came in and were all beat to hell, then I finally realized it was Thanksgiving. Ha, what a joke there would be no giving thanks in that crazy place. I started to think a lot about my personal safety at this point and found myself saying (out loud sometimes) "I want to live. I want to live.".

My morale at that time was shaken but still remained pretty high. Most likely due to the fraternity calendar Donna sent me with her picture in it that I immediately hung on the wall of my bunker above my dirty ass pillow. She was so beautiful, a combination of sweet and sexy at the same time. She absolutely made me want to be home more than I already did.

Just after Thanksgiving we took another trip up to Happy Valley and went back to the Ho Chi Hilton. This time we found 6000 pounds of rice, many of the bags were actually from the U.S. our special gift to the VC apparently! We also found clothes, rain gear and ammo. It was another good find and a real hit to the VC, but it was a hairy experience going up that narrow trail where we were completely exposed to ambush.

We wounded a VC in the back as they withdrew from their position at the Ho Chi Hilton and one of my squad leaders, LaPree was slightly wounded as well. A booby trap got him. The reaction squad brought us some C-4 and thermite grenades which we used to burn all the baskets of rice with, the bagged rice we just opened and dumped in the river into the stream that flowed next to the trail.

I was more afraid that day than I had been in quite a while. My men were spread out all over the side of the ridge and Charles was jamming our radio. I was sure at any second that we were going to get hit hard and the suspense was just prolonged when LaPree got wounded and we had to take him down to the valley floor to medevac him. We had to cross the river again and then go back up with the C-4 and thermite. But luckily, I got my men out there with LaPree being the only casualty. I held my nervousness close to my chest that day so the men wouldn't get overly concerned but I was concerned shitless on the inside.

On the patrol back to base camp we shot at three VC and one of them dropped a canister he was carrying. I don't think we killed any of them though. We broke up into three ambushes for the night and I went with third squad this time. I had on a rain suit and poncho and even though it rained most of the night I was actually pretty comfortable. The only place the bugs could get at me was my face and even though I covered myself in bug repellent they still came after me pretty good.

We hooked back up with first and second squad shortly after first light and made it back in around 0745. We got in early enough, so I took a pan bath, shaved and went down and had a pretty good breakfast of sausage and eggs. It was always nice to get a hot meal in your belly when you could.

From time to time, I would get scoop on the whereabouts of my classmates from OCS and The Basic School. Sam Hall stopped by on a M-16 inspection tour and is now working with G4, he told me that Murphy was going to G5 and Pinckert left two days ago for division schools. I was glad to hear they were all out of the field safe, but it made me hope more I could get through the next 1-2 months alive and get home safe.

Apparently, I was making an impression
with my superiors by this time and on
December 4th the Skipper asked me If I
wanted to be General Robinson's aide.
Colonel Davis came out for an inspection and
told me personally he would be
recommending me for the job. It was hard to
believe when I heard the word come out of
his mouth. I would be in the rear with the
gear! No more getting shot at and I would
almost surely go home alive and in one piece.

No matter what though I only had six more weeks in the field max at this point.

I also got the report on December 4th from the airstrike I had called in on November 18th we killed 14 VC wounded eight and destroyed one 82mm mortar tube. We got this information from a VC courier who was captured, along with a trove of intelligence from some found VC documents he had on him. I have to say I was happy about the report, but it still didn't change our day to day, or the fact that I wanted to kill Charles every day.

We had been running ambush patrols regularly under the new Skipper. Gannon called him "Captain Blitzkrieg" and at this point he was still trying to change everything and was little more than a bundle of nervous energy.

We got a chance to go into Da Nang on December 6th with Pete Millsap, Jack Smith, Dave Harris, and MacPherson. We met up with Captain Meyers and boy what a night we had getting drunk at the Stone Elephant and MAC V clubs. We made it to the Korean Club later. It was off limits to us but it was a good time and we knew it so we would take the risk if we had the opportunity. That night though the club got raided by the MP's and we had to run out the back, climb up on the roof and hide from them so we wouldn't get caught. We waited a while and then jumped down after we figured they were gone. Scared the crap out of an enlisted man when we jumped down. Da Nang was a wild time. It is funny to me looking back how many times I should have gotten busted, but I guess I always had the luck of the Irish on my side and never did.

CHAPTER 21
PHUOC "FUCK" NINH
A heroic day of loss

Christmas time in the field may be the worst time in a Marine's life. It is a constant reminder of loved ones and things you are missing back home. Even though I was getting packages left and right I was still pretty depressed. Mom sent a bottle of whiskey and a Christmas tree that we set up in the bunker and put a bunch of presents for GTO under. I got several sexy letters from Donna and Connie, who said she is ready to go back to Mexico with me. Jim and Mary Weir sent me a fantastic box filled with soap, powder, socks, cookies and the like and Judy sent me an instamatic 104 that I used to take a lot of the pictures you are seeing in this book. I even got some brownies from a girl named Robin whom I didn't even know, which I thought was nice. They tasted fantastic and we promptly downed them all with some beers. Hell, Grandpa even sent me his usual $5 for Christmas. He is just too much, and he will never know how much that $5 meant to me sitting in that dark, rainy jungle hell.

I took that instamatic out on an ambush patrol on December 16th with the new Lieutenant Paul Skoog. I broke off with Smedley's squad and set up in our ambush site that night. Around 0445 Doc Lucas woke me up and pointed out an NVA unit moving behind our ambush site into Happy Valley.

They looked very military-like because they were NVA. We lit them up with grenades, three law rockets, many rounds from the M16s and even threw in some M79 rounds for good measure. As I threw my first grenade I leaned down and whispered to Lt Skoog, the new Lt, "It's like this every night!" The NVA unit scattered and ran and we did not get a casualty count and we left our ambush site rather quickly.

We met back up with Sargent's Lambert, Healey and the rest of the squads the following morning and really tore the hell out of Phuc Ninh, which all the troops called "Fuck" Ninh. Blew up some caves and at least did some good for troop morale. I was glad to see that troop morale was high since this time of year can really drag the men down but I was feeling down, and all the rain, bugs and rice paddies were just making it worse.

I was tired of my present job, patrolling and ambushes were getting old and boring. I couldn't help but feel that my luck in the field was ready to run out. I even put in for an AO spot and was still waiting on word

about the aide position for General Robinson.
As luck would have it though, just when I
was feeling my darkest, we drew cards that
night and my platoon was selected from the
battalion to see the Bob Hope show on
December 18. We were on an ambush the
night before and we humped in from the
ambush to hill 10. We grabbed some chow,
didn't shower, and then we all humped down
to Highway1. about a mile from the hill.
Without our own transportation, we managed
to hitch a ride, picking up GTO on the way,
and made it to the show just as it was
starting. Raquel Welch was on stage.

We saw that all the seats were occupied by the rear guys who were dressed in their summer best uniforms. We looked like shit and smelled like high heaven, and we managed to force our way to the front. It wasn't much of a problem since we were in full combat gear. Even GTO looked like a little marine. At the very front I see Major Larsen, who, as it turns out, enlisted me in the Corps. I told him that I knew Raquel Welch from San Diego. I was put up on the stage with her and she came rushing over to me but when she got within 2 feet of me, she jumped back. I realize it was my stink because she replies and I apologize but she was kind enough to give me a hug.

The 20th of December would be a day that would forever change my life and a day that I could never forget no matter how hard I tried, how many beers I drank or what path life took me down in the future to come. The brutality of that day was something no training could ever prepare you for and no counselor, doctor or psychiatrist would ever be able to fix after it happened. It would just be something that haunted me for the rest of my life.

The night of the 20th would be long, hard, loud, and bloody. By this time, I was given a lot of latitude planning my patrols and ambushes. Like other members of our company, I strongly felt there were too many VC and NVA in the area. This later proved to be quite true as they were preparing for Tet, which happened a few weeks later. I presented my plan to company and battalion and they okayed it. My plan was to go out to the mouth of Mortar Valley, where the Phouc Ninh villages were located. Each one had a separate numerical number, and I wanted to set up my CP in Phouc Ninh 5. My Marines all pronounced it as "Fuck" Ninh trying to use the word fuck as often as possible. I wanted to send out three ambushes on trails we knew were frequently used by the enemy. I had personally seen the footprints, and knew these trails had potential. We had passed this information up the chain of command, but no action was taken to increase the regimental activity in the area.

I took my platoon out that night and we set up in Phouc Ninh 5 initially. We moved in silently, and after surrounding the village we entered quietly and took the villagers by surprise. I had a Chu Hoi with me. (Chu Hoi were former VC who served as advisors to us). He had been with me on occasions before. We wanted to get as much information from the villagers as possible. It was an NVA/VC village, and there were several pregnant women. I remember seeing our Chu Hoi squeezing the knuckles of a young boy, maybe eight or nine, as they both squatted side-by-side. He was trying to extract information from him. The boy had tears streaming down his cheeks. I did not interfere, as any of the information obtained might be very valuable and save a Marine's life. In any other situation, I would have stopped it. I never allowed torture for torture's sake. But this was not a usual stop in a village.

I felt that we were going to see some action that night, little did I know what was to come. After we had been in the village for some time, I sent out my three squads, my squad leaders were Cpls. Pettit, Kurtz and Smedley. I only had two machine guns with me that night, as generally we were limited to two machine guns per platoon. Since Smedley's squad consisted of only six Marines, I set up his squad's ambush on a trail that I felt was the least likely for the enemy to use. and each of the other squads a machine gun each.

I remained behind with 12 Marines, including my ARTY FO Lt Chris Christensen and Sgt Lambert and the 60 mortars, to guard the village (actually we functioned as a 4th ambush site) . I knew could better coordinate everything from the village anyway.

The night was quiet with radio checks indicating nothing to report. I was on the platoon radio, when suddenly, Smedley came up on the net. He whispered in a very low voice, that over 100 VC had just gone by his position and more were coming. I immediately relayed the info to our company CP.

As I recall, our CO and I talked directly. I asked him to notify battalion so the ARTY would be set to shoot my prearranged artillery fires that I had scheduled in the event we made contact. I also asked him to activate the reaction platoon and get it going out to us. This just took a few seconds, and then I ordered the other 2 squads to prepare to move out to our prearranged rendezvous point. I then said to Smedley, "shoot them." The entire sky lit up with tracer rounds and the sound of M-16 fire filled the air.

I moved out of the village with five Marines, including Christensen. I left Sgt. Lambert behind with the 60-mortar team to guard the village. I told Smedley to get the hell out of their ambush site and link up with us at the rendezvous point where the other two squads were also moving. Believe me, moving out, in pure darkness, with no moon, with three different squads moving from different directions was a difficult maneuver. Also, I knew a reaction squad was heading out to join us, led by Chris Gannon, another platoon commander. Eventually we were all able to link up at the rendezvous point.

At one point during the link up one of the squads who I linked up with on the way to the rendezvous point told me they saw some enemy off to our left and wanted to open fire. I moved up, and since I could not positively ID them as VC, I would not let my marines shoot and we kept moving towards the rendezvous site. I must say that one of the greatest fears you have in a fluid combat situation where you have several separate small units moving to link up in absolute darkness is shooting friendlies.

My 3 squads and my group arrived at the rendezvous site all within minutes of each other. We knew the area well, and I had picked a site that we all knew from past patrols. Gannon and his reaction squad arrived almost soon thereafter. I sent them to check out an area I thought some of the enemy had gone to, and then I took my platoon headed towards the area where Smedley thought the main force of VC had scattered. All the while on the radio now with Bn we gave chase and after about 300 meters, we were hit with what I thought were mortars, LAWS, grenades, machine guns and small arms fire. I ordered my platoon forward and we attacked them. Our position when they opened fire on us was indefensible! We fought like hell for at least 30 minutes, but it seemed much longer.

Finally, the enemy fire dwindled down and we were surrounded but we were in a tight perimeter. We were still receiving enemy fire but much less. I asked for a casualty report and I was told that we had about five wounded. A machine gunner named Bobian was KIA and I heard that

Smedley was presumed dead but they had not found his body. I recalled seeing him leading his squad forward as we attacked the ambushing enemy. I wanted his body found and made it clear we had to find it before the enemy did. His body was eventually located and brought into the circle that we had made to defend ourselves.

We were taking a lot of hand grenades inside of our perimeter. I was worried that our wounded would be hit by one of the grenades. I took off my flak jacket and laid it on top of one of the wounded Marines. I then had my marines take off their flak jackets so we were able to completely cover all of our wounded.

Kurtz, one of my squad leaders, was badly wounded and he looked like he had lost at least part of his shooting hand. We quickly got morphine in all of them and this quieted them down. I kept moving around inside the perimeter with Cpl. Dohanish, my radioman. At one point in time, he said to me, "Sir every time you yell, they shoot at us." Since he was tethered to me by a very short line, and I had the radio phone constantly in my

ear, he did have cause for concern if they
shot at me!

There was a ridge line about 30-40
meters in front of us and at some point, I
started receiving fire from it. The bullets
were hitting all around me and no wonder my
radioman was worried! I yelled to Cpl Petit
to get his squad up there and kill those
bastards. Petit's squad took off up the incline
yelling like a bunch of wild Indians and
killed or scattered the bad guys.

290

I went over to check on our wounded. Smedley's body had been found in the dense brush and brought into our perimeter. In addition to Kurtz and Jackson, Kuykendall and Hardy were also wounded. All this was communicated to Bn and a medevac was called. All this time we are still virtually surrounded, receiving grenades and small arms fire and sporadic machine gun fire. I could not understand why the enemy was so persistent. Generally, once any shooting started, they would break away and high tail it out of the area.

I grabbed Kurtz's M-79 and his M79 rounds and went after a VC Machine Gunner. I fired several rounds at him and then grabbed some grenades and I was sneaking down to throw them when this gook stuck his head up a few feet in front of me. Shocked the hell out of me and I quickly dropped the grenades and shot him with my 45.

Then, in the darkness I saw what I thought initially was a .106 barrel. It later turned out to be a rocket launching tube and the reason the enemy was fighting so hard— they wanted them back!

We continued to take more incoming grenades and small arms fire for the next 2 hours. In the interim, Hill 10 got hit with mortars (probably to draw attention away from the pre-planned rocket attack that we had interrupted.

This weapon was captured approximately 10 miles south west of Danang on 21 December 1967 by Company "D", 1st Battalion, 7th Marine Regiment, 1st Marine Division, and is the first such weapons captured in South Vietnam.

We got good arty support, and Christensen, the arty FO, did an excellent job calling it in. I was told that Puff the Magic Dragon, (a C130 loaded with high velocity machine guns that could set down a huge wall of fire, was on station to give us support). I did not want Puff too close-having seen the wall of fire they could put out. I directed him a click away into Mortar Valley to hit the enemy with more force than they had ever seen!

292

At this point, a medevac showed up, but he received so much enemy fire that I told him it was a no go. He was a good pilot. (I later met him when I became an AO) I checked with my corpsmen and I was told that at least one of our wounded might die if we did not get them out to medical care. I was on the radio with the pilot, who insisted on waiting around upstairs . I told him about the critical situation for at least one wounded Marine. He said he was coming in and we guided him in, and the enemy really opened up on him. We did the best to suppress the firing and we quickly put the wounded on the chopper and it took off. How the pilot was able to take off and land in the hail of enemy fire is still a mystery to me.

I helped carry the dead and wounded down to the medevac site which was outside of our perimeter.
On the way back I suddenly felt a hand reach out of the brush. It was a VC grabbing for me. Shocked the hell out of me, and I shot him with my M16 and then I jumped on him and stabbed him several times with my knife. Kept stabbing him until I heard the sound of

air hissing out of his lungs. Once I knew he was dead, I returned to the perimeter.

This was the first and only time I ever killed a man with my K Bar. I went back at first light and searched for his body and found his wallet with a picture of his wife and son in it. As I recall, he was an NVA from Hanoi.

We had previously tightened our perimeter and we also found another complete rocket launcher including the tripod—not just the tube. We waited for the sun to come up—it seemed to take forever! Finally, the sun came up-so did Rich Gannon and his platoon, a welcome sight!

It was the longest night of my life. I will never forget the sound of the spoons falling off the grenades. Searching the area, we found 9 enemy dead plus plenty of blood trails, weapons, a machine gun, and grenades, etc.

Christmas was a pretty bleak day that year, but I did bring up GTO and gave him his presents so there was a little joy. He stayed the night and I got drunk as hell on the whiskey my Mom sent to me. They told me the next morning I was trying to knock down the wall in one of the tents. It was just me dealing with what had happened to Smedley in the only way I knew how at the time. I will never forget my squad leader and he will always be remembered for his actions that day and the lives he saved. I received the Navy Cross for my actions that night and Smedley received the Congressional Medal of Honor.

CHAPTER 22
Goodbye Hill 41
Hello Marble Mountain

I found out on December 28th I was accepted to AO school. It was my understanding that every 2nd Lieutenant in the 1st Marine Division volunteered to be in the AO program. Seven of us went in for interviews at Division on the 27th and I was one of the lucky ones to grab a spot. I did get to see Pinckert and Sam Hall while I was heading to the interview and caught Murphy on his way to R&R as well, so it was a good day all around.

I came back to Hill 41 and got orders to report to Marble Mountain for AO school on January 3rd. My days on the Hill now had a number and that was fine by me. Plus, I would make more money so that was a bonus. I would miss the men in my platoon, but I was going to lose it in January anyway. With only seven months to go it was hard to believe things were looking up in a place with very little positive aspects.

I was convinced the year to come would have to be better than the last one. I had suffered through a bitter winter in Quantico, mostly outdoors training, and then six months in Vietnam watching my men die in front of me and fighting for my life in a war I knew we could not win by fighting with the tactics we were using. I knew when I left this place, I would forever feel as if I had a new lease on life.

On January 2nd I shook hands and bid farewell to all of those I could, and surprisingly, had to fight back some tears along the way before heading over to Hill 10. Some of these men had saved my life with their actions, and some would never make it home, and I knew that, as I shook their hands goodbye. I knew a little something about each of these men that only men who have come close to death together can know about each other. They would forever be my men, and more importantly, my comrades in arms. In a strange way I felt almost as if I was deserting them, but it was time to move on and give myself a shot at making it through this war. I knew that I had taught them a lot and I hoped that I had inspired them to be good Marines. their fate was now based more in luck than skill.

Of course, in a true demonstration of how this war really put you on edge every second of every day as I spent my last two days in the field, we were attacked, hard and heavy. On the morning of January 3rd, I had just hit the rack following a great John Wayne movie. I hadn't had a drink for a week at that point. I was feeling clear headed and excited for my upcoming change of pace. About 0100 we were mortared, and of course all the Lieutenants dove into the hole directly in front of our hooch. I was the second one in diving headfirst wearing only my long johns and carrying my M-16. I was really concerned and kept praying no rounds would hit our small hole that was quickly loaded up with eight men.

They overran the MAC V compound down the road and ambushed our reactionary force as well. Hitting three tanks with RPG's and wounding several men. Then around 0400 they hit Da Nang with rockets from over near the Bo Ban river area. It really pissed us off to know that they had snuck into our area and fired rockets at Da Nang. But our 106's and 81's were quick to return a pretty accurate volley of their own rounds and the next morning we found 22 unfired rockets and three dead VC. Dave Harris was wounded in the leg leading the reactionary force out, but he would be okay. It all just made me want to leave for Marble Mountain faster, which I did on January 4th.

When I got there, I first had to report to 1st Marine division AO unit which was in the S-2 Section of the Division command group. I reported to a Major in S-2

After reporting to Division, I was driven over to Marble Mountain by one of the drivers. My first view of Marble Mountain was something else. There were individual Quonset huts set aside for the pilots close to the Officer's Club and another for the enlisted crews in a different area. The Officer section was also closer to the beach on the shore of the South China Sea. I was introduced to the CO of the AO unit, Major Wanner and several of the other AO's. I got set up in one of the AO hooch's right on the main street.

Wow, what a set-up it was for this place, especially considering what I was used to by this point. They had a really nice Club, fantastic chow, and maids. Fucking maids! The first day I made some new friends and we played some touch football on the beach. It was a blast to just relax and not worry about getting shot just walking around for once, but it really reminded me of California and how much I missed home.

I will never forget my first evening chow at Marble Mountain. I lined up for evening chow like normal and behind me were two other pilots complaining about the fact that we were having steak again. I was astounded at their complaints. I ate two steaks that night and so much ice cream I threw up. Yep, I was in heaven.

The next day we started what we called our OJT AO school. There was of course a formal AO school in North Carolina and I recall it was a three-month long course. We were told we would be brought up to speed in two weeks. We already had an advantage by having been on the ground and knowing about combat firsthand. What we didn't know was how to function as an AO. Learning how to use the radios was probably the hardest aspect of the training. Using them to coordinate with the aircraft that we had to control was quite a task. The artillery aspect was much easier for us since most of us already had a lot of experience calling for fire on the ground from our supporting artillery batteries. The demand from the air was something completely different though but would become much easier once we started flying.

Our main instructor in our OJT school was Jim Sanders. He was a great guy, formerly an enlisted man, he was very knowledgeable and gruff just like you would expect any old salty dog to be. He took his time with us, but we still progressed quite rapidly. Probably much faster than anyone thought we could. Although I do vividly remember getting my ass chewed out by Major Wanner, no less over the net, during one of my first flights because I was not properly monitoring all three of my radios. I did not realize that what was being sent over the radio was something I needed to respond too. He taught me quickly! Our training was fantastic.

One the best things about the unit was that the other more experienced AO's did not Lord their experience over us. They welcomed us and supported us since they really needed the support themselves. There were four of us new guys which brought the unit total up to a whopping 13 men including Major Wanner, so small mistakes aside we were welcomed by everyone.

The big advantage we had as officers was that we had a chance to question the other AO's after we got off for the day over a few drinks. We would learn a lot from them and the other pilots, mostly helicopter pilots, over many drinks.

Early on, I met the helicopter pilot who evacuated my wounded during the 20 December shoot up, and he was a good guy. I had put him up for a Silver Star and I heard he received it a little bit later. I told him personally that what he did was one of the bravest things I had ever seen in my life. We had many drinks together after that at the club when we weren't flying.

There were three other new AO's aside from myself, Mike Hendrickson, Bill Coleman and Bob Disney. Stu Berman was also an AO and had formerly been with our battalion but were never with our company. He had been a platoon commander with 1/7 but I had never spent much time with him and didn't really know him beyond facial recognition at that point. That would all change quickly as we all became close within the AO unit almost from the start. Several of the AO's were former enlisted men like Pappy, Lippe and Sanders. The rest of us were newly arrived Lieutenants. We all had our flight physicals the next day, and as usual had to lay down to get my blood pressure down. I had a prostate infection at the time, and it hurt like hell. Luckily, I passed the physical, so I got four hours of flight time on January 9th looking for a downed CH-53 helicopter that was carrying 35 men when it went down. I found out later there was actually a Marine Corps General on board as well. Which explained why so many planes were out looking for the downed chopper and why I was even flying a mission at all, at this point. We had no luck finding them and would later learn when they finally found the downed helicopter that all on board were KIA.

It was an interesting first experience to say the least for my first mission in a O-1 Charlie (Also known as the Cessna L-19/O-1 Bird Dog). During the Vietnam War, the Bird Dog was Primarily for reconnaissance, target acquisition, adjusting artillery, radio relay, and escorting convoys. I flew with Captain Greb and we set down in Phu Bai to refuel along the way. He taught me a lot as I settled into my job as an AO. Basically though, we were just feet to the fire learning new things every day for the first month or two. He was very clearly a career Marine

It would be a while before we were really allowed to fly on all our missions with our pilot counterparts. It was a precarious set up in the O-1 Bird Dog. The plane was a two-person set up with the AO sitting in the backseat, which he had to cram into first. I learned early that we always set on our parachutes and never actually wore them. It was basically impossible to bail out of an O-1 Bird Dog, because the pilot got in last and would obviously be first out leaving no way for the AO to exit the plane in time. So, the unwritten rule was, that the pilot would not wear his parachute either and if we had to go down, we would go down together. This rule was, for the most part, unspoken, but clearly understood by all of us.

The O-1 Bird Dog was basically a WWII aircraft, with an overhead wing, single engine and was relatively easy to land, even if it was hit. The backseat also had a place in the floor of the aircraft to place a flying stick so the AO could fly the plane from the back seat in case of emergency. There were also pedals on the floorboard of the aircraft, both left and right, that controlled the attitude of the plane. It wasn't too hard to surmise that in this confined and very basic aircraft the lives of the two people inside literally depended on each other with every mission.

We flew most of our missions with Army pilots, who were very good about teaching us how to fly the plane, because they knew if they were to get hit by enemy fire on one of our rocket runs to mark a target that it would be the AO in the backseat who would have to bring back the plane or crash land. Like I said before, if one of us was going down we were both going down. That's just the way it was, period. In fact, shortly before I arrived at Marble Mountain an AO had to crash land an aircraft from the backseat because his pilot was badly wounded by enemy fire. Luckily, he was trained well just as we would be.

I got to see a Korean floor show on January 15th and boy did we get destroyed in the process. I was buying 10 beers at a time and I even got up on the stage and danced with this sexy Korean gal. Then we went to an after party in one of the 34 pilot's hooch's and I drank gin and rum straight with Mike Barksdale. Finally crawled into my rack and passed out with my boots on, Christ, did I feel like hell the next day. I went outside my hooch and found Barksdale passed out in the sand outside. He never even made it back to his hooch.

I did finally get some mail though and got some pictures from Mom so that helped me feel a little better and I finally got over that pesky prostate gland infection as well. Not a bad day despite the hangover.

The next day I got to fly with Captain Greb again and we buzzed my old stomping grounds on Hill 41 to air drop some magazines. Talked to Perkins on the radio as we did, and he told me he would be coming home on the 27th. I was happy about that but then he told me that Major U'ren the 1/7 S2 tripped a booby trap and lost his foot. I sure was glad I was out of there and only had six more months to go in Vietnam.

One of the best parts of being in the rear as an AO was just the fact that you got to relax. Because of the intensity of our time in the air we tried to take advantage of our time on the ground but when we worked, we worked hard.

I remember sitting outside of our hooch just catching rays and enjoying the sun like I did back in California. I would get to see my friends a lot as they came in from the field for R&R or for schools and such. Sometimes they would show and sometimes they wouldn't but that was the Marine Corps for you. There was even a floor show about once a month at the Officers Club. If I recall correctly, beer was a nickel and a bottle of champagne cost $.50. Needless to say, we frequently woke up with serious hangovers, but they never really bothered us when it came time to fly because it was our job to help the troops on the ground.

Whenever we flew from the start of my time as an AO to the very end, I would try to bring magazines, newspapers and tabasco sauce to drop to the troops on the ground. It was the least I could do knowing how bad it was in the field. I was very conscious at the time that I only had six months to go.

Ken Mott left to go back to the world (what Marines at war call the home) on January 23rd that old "Kahuna" was a good guy. He did a lot as the O Club manager, having redone the entire club so it was nice and beautiful with a view of the beach and all with windows facing the South China Sea beyond the massive stacks of barbed wire piled up to protect the base. I was going to miss him, but I was glad he got out safe and sound.

We always walked around armed and if the VC ever tried to come into our base, I knew we would defend that club to the last man. I was surely sad to see Mott go but Sigler flew in a few days before that and said he would be back on the 10th of February, so I knew that I had a hell of a party to look forward to.

We used a lot of slang in Vietnam and Marines continue to use much of that slang today as they develop their own. At one point I thought it would be fun to catalog some of the words we used for fun and realized how much we used overall. The troops, myself included, would say things like "You're a little flakey" which meant don't bullshit me. "I might but I kind of doubt it." "You're all ate up with the dumbass." "Can you dig it?" "Zipperhead" "Slopehead" "Round-eyes" "That's his bag" "Face" and that was just a few of the terms we used at the time. Many of the troops came from poor educational backgrounds and their general English skills were lacking but they were very vivid, and I was quite fascinated with how they expressed themselves. It seemed to make it easier to get along coming from different backgrounds, as we all did. I think at some point every Marine learns that it's not really a sentence if it doesn't contain the word fuck. Young Marines learn the art of swearing from the seasoned Gunny's in some of the most descriptive ways. And when I was with the troops, much like the other officers, we all talked the same way.

I wasn't blind to the fact that many of our slang words were derogatory towards our enemy, the native people of Vietnam, and Asia in general. But that is the head space you must be in ,as a Marine at war. You can't take the time facing the split-second decisions you have to make in an ambush to humanize the people shooting at you on the other side, or you die, literally.

The sad part about that is that It becomes a state of mind while you are there and continues when you come out of the field and when you go back to the real world.

Being in the rear as an AO and so close to Da Nang was great but it really was easy

311

to go out and get drunker than hell. In fact, after one particular drunken night with Stu Berman and John Disney where we wound up at some whore house drinking with some ARVN's who then drove us around searching for girls. I decided that I had to knock it off for a while. There had been to many terrorist attacks in lately and it was like I was leading a three-man drunk patrol through the back alleys and just looking for trouble. Later we would realize that the enemy were probing our defenses around in anticipation of the Tet offensive.

I did hold true to my promise, at least for a few days but on January 27th, I went into Da Nang with Mike Barksdale, Pete Millichap and a few other guys. We all went to a Korean Club to have some drinks and watch the floor show. Pete and I cut out soon after we got there to go find Cpl. Beckford and his Filipino buddies. Beckford, who worked for Millichap in the civil affairs section of my old battalion was invaluable to our group, as he spoke fluent Vietnamese.

As luck would have it during what would become known as the Tet offensive, I was invited by Cpl. Beckford and Pete Millichap to go on a recon patrol and find some trouble get into for the night. It was a good night even though I had to pay for Beckford who was broke as usual. At 0700 we went back to the Filipino place and started drinking again. By 1000 we were all shit faced and started shooting the coconuts off the tree in their front yard with our .45's. Of course, we accidentally shot their electrical line which cut the power to their house and the great music they had going. Needless to say, it really brought the party down.

So, Beckford and I went around the corner to Missy Ohm's house, and she called up one of her girlfriends for me. We ended up having a very nice dinner at a home in an area of town where a lot of Filipino workers stayed that worked for USAID. At the dinner I was seated opposite Missy Ohm's friend she had arranged for me, a beautiful Vietnamese widow named Wai. She was the epitome of Vietnamese beauty. She wore the traditional dress of a Lady and didn't look at all like the village women that I had seen

313

when I was a grunt. I immediately fell in love. We had done a lot of drinking before arriving for the dinner, and I was a little obvious looking at her across the table like I was smitten.

We initially ate what I thought to be chicken but would later be informed was fried dog. There were several courses during the meal that I still cannot begin to describe. They were so foreign to me. At one point an egg was placed in front of us that seemed to have been boiled. I observed and copied the others at the table in their manners and tapped my egg open revealing a cooked baby chick inside. I told Beckford "I can't eat that" and Beckford in turn told Wai what I had said in Vietnamese. She told him if I did eat it, she would go to bed with me. I jammed the egg into my mouth so fast I almost choked on it but eventually got it down.   Later that evening she would take me next door where we would spend the night together. Wai had a baby boy who was maybe two years old as well as a live-in maid. Her deceased husband was apparently a Vietnamese Marine who died in combat. We spent a beautiful night making love. She was unlike any other woman I had met in Vietnam.

The next morning, I decided I would just spend another day with her even though I was supposed to go back to the AO unit. I managed to get a message to someone in the unit and the guys helped cover for me. We spent the day getting to know some of the Filipinos in the area and I remember her maid killing a live chicken in the backyard, which she then cooked for dinner. I spent the rest of the night making love to the beautiful Wai.

As we lay sleeping in the early hours of the morning, I would say around 4a.m. I heard a lot of what I thought were firecrackers going off. Little did I know but the Tet Offensive had just begun. Some Filipino workers pounded on Wai's door and alerted me to what was going on. I quickly got dressed, grabbed my .45, and started off though the streets making my way back to friendly territory. I didn't know the area well but at least I knew which direction I had to go to get across the river and back to Marble Mountain.

After what seemed like quite a while, but in all likelihood was just a few minutes, a Jeep with two Marines in it came careening around the corner and I promptly jumped out in front of it waving them down just before they ran me over. They were of course shocked to see me given what was going on, quickly waved me into the Jeep and beat a hasty retreat. We were terrified that we would be captured by the enemy as we made our way back to Marble Mountain. We passed several dead bodies on the streets as we maneuvered our way back and at one point, I counted at least 17 dead VC in what was obviously the sight of a heavy firefight earlier.

We finally reached Marine lines. Never had I been so glad to see my fellow Marines in my life. I had never felt more naked or in danger than I had while sneaking through the streets armed with only my .45 and my wits. I hopped a ferry across the river to the Marble Mountain side and got back onboard base with my fellow AO's who really went out of their way to cover for me. I got zero shit for being gone for two days at all. I got there

around 0730 just in time for my 0800
Mohawk flight even though I was dodging
dead bodies most of the way.

Of course, we had also just been hit by
mortars in the morning and the following
morning we got hit by 140mm rockets.
Damage was relatively light both nights. We
lost a couple of helicopters and had a few
KIA's as well. We were on alert for most of
the next week following Tet and on February
6th we got word that two regiments of NVA
were supposed to hit and everyone was on
edge. I did however have an M-79 and my
trusty .45 at the ready just in case.

On February 1st I flew in an O-1 with an
Army pilot. We ran two flights of fixed wing
flights in a bunker position. We were told to
go out and the fixed wing would be waiting
for us at this known VC position. After
running those two flights of bombs on target,
a VC staggered out of one of the bunkers. It
was obvious that he was shellshocked from
the bombing, but he looked otherwise
unharmed. I convinced the pilot to make a
pass on the VC at a very low altitude so I
could shoot at him with my M-16.

Now trust me when I say that shooting someone from an airplane on the move is not easy, especially when they are staggering around from shell shock. Although I was a pretty good shot and still am, it took several passes and probably 70 rounds of ammunition before I ended up putting a bullet in his back. He fell to the ground and immediately you could see a big red patch of blood expanding on his light blue shirt slowly turning the entire shirt red. I assumed that the shot was fatal, but we circled for a while to ensure he did not move. I now had my first confirmed M-16 kill from the air!

Not surprisingly the heavy drinking continued that night. Not sure whether to blame Sigler and Barksdale for being a bad influence on me or myself for trying to dampen my own bewilderment and growing sickness for this war we were fighting the wrong way. Take out the political agendas and we could win this war in a week.

I got almost eight hours of flight time on February 5th with the Air Force, even tried to catch the new James Bond flick "You Only Live Twice" between flights but of course a rocket attack cleared out the movie and that was that.

I was starting to get good flight time now and on February 13th I witnessed my first air strike from an aerial position. I was flying for the Army and we called in one flight of fixed wing and some Huey's on a VC unit that had some Marines from Mike 3/7 pinned down. They were also using mortars on the Marines, but we were unable to spot the launch tube flashes to call fire on them. This had been my first real chance to work with ground units and in all honesty, it was a little sad because the Marines had taken so many casualties. Even though I knew they lost a lot of men it made me feel good that we could help them out and I started to realize just how important what I was doing was to the lives of our troops on the ground.

On February 11th I got to fly at night for over eight hours and got some stick time in an O-2 aircraft. We called the O-2 a push pull because it had two engines, one in front and one behind. It was an Air Force plane we flew on the few occasions we did end up flying with Air Force pilots. Interestingly there was a Marine Major on assignment with the Air Force and quite often we would fly with him. He was a great guy and taught me a lot personally. On this night since we flew for over eight hours, he let me fly more than I ever had before. We were basically flying a circle around and then along the coast toward the city of Hoi An.

There was a beacon light that I somehow got fixated on while the Major was sleeping. He woke up just in time to grab the controls from me and pull us out of the dive that I had the plane in…we were heading straight toward the ground. It was a strange sensation that overcame me, and the pilot quickly told me that I had vertigo and that is what caused me to be hypnotized by the beacon light. He was such a good guy and had obviously seen the issue before, so he didn't even bother chewing me out for almost killing us both. He was as calm as could be, told me that it could happen to the best of pilots given the right circumstances and even let me fly some more that night.

The O-2 was a totally different plan than the O-1 Bird Dog. The O-2 was a push-pull aircraft that had two propellers behind the cockpit. It had a better range than the O-1 and could fly longer before refueling. The AO and the pilot also sat side by side in the O-2, which was more comfortable, but the O-1 was far superior to control other aircraft and work simultaneously with the ground assets since it had an overhead wing, which allowed you to see the ground assets better, and there were also a few other small advantages to the 0-1's operation. Bottom line was the AO's preferred the O-1 by far.

I made 1st LT on the 12th of February but couldn't go into Da Nang to celebrate because some idiot Army dude backed his truck up into our jeep while I was driving it and completely totaled the jeep, tipping it over and throwing me to the ground. I had to scramble out of the way and was lucky the jeep didn't roll over on me. I felt bad about the whole thing even though it wasn't my fault because it left us with no transportation for the entire AO unit. So instead of going into Da Nang, I got drunk and acted like a wild man with Sigler. Who got there on February 10th. Man did we act like idiots, tearing apart the hooch, breaking bottles and turning over dressers. It was a crazy night, but it was good to see my old friend and it was one of those odd bonding moments you only get in a combat zone. I had been drinking too much lately and really needed to dial it back for a while. I needed an R and R and it couldn't come soon enough.

I put in for R and R in Australia, but honestly, at that point anywhere would have been better than Vietnam. I missed the beautiful round-eyed women of the western world.

It was February 14th when I learned that my old platoon had been ambushed on the first day of Tet. Sgt. Lambert, my old platoon Sgt., was wounded badly and had to be medivaced out. Doc Stull was killed along with one of my radio operators and several others. I would later hear that the Lieutenant that replaced me was also killed fighting alongside the members of my old platoon. I knew the area where the ambush took place well. It was close to the main road and just up from hill 41 and was usually extremely safe and secure. I doubt that things would have been different if I had been there although in my mind, I somehow thought they would have been.

I spent many restless nights after that thinking about the fine men that died that day in the ambush and whether or not I could have prevented any of it at all. I even wrote to Sgt. Lambert's home address and sent some pictures that I had taken of the platoon. At that point in time, I didn't even know if he was dead or alive, I only knew he had been badly wounded in the ass.

One of the nicer things about being at Marble Mountain was you could just sit out and catch some sun, maybe write some letters to friends and family back home and not have to worry about a sniper putting one in your melon. I was writing home more these days and got some letters myself from women I had almost forgotten about, like a stew that I used to date back in D.C. It all just made me want that Australia R and R more than ever. But in the time being we just passed the time by flying missions and drinking more and more.

I organized a big party with the Catkillers, the Army unit we flew with on February 25th. The Marine unit call signs were all "Cowpoke" followed by a designation number; I was "Cowpoke 23" for example. I had a new role in the AO unit. I figured out that the division thought AO's were taken care of by the wing and conversely the wing assumed that the division took care of us.

We were under the division command and that was who should have supported us but there was no procedure in place to do so. So, starting that day and each month thereafter, I would go to division and complain that the wing had not given us our share of steaks or beer for the month. Since there was no method of cross reference, or record keeping at all, for that matter, I would go to the wing and do the same thing. I worked the system to get us double portions of beer and steaks, what a coup. We would party right there on the beach outside the wire on the shores of the South China Sea. Today you will find mostly hotels in that spot, but the sand is still the same and the view is just as beautiful.

But the good times never lasted in Vietnam and I got a letter the same day from Sgt. Lambert letting me know that Doc Stull had in fact been killed. It really hit me hard as I had Doc Stull from the day, he joined the company until the day I went to Marble Mountain. He was a really good man and part of me wondered if you would have made it out had I still been there with the men. He would always have aspirin and extra toilet paper for me in the field. It was the little stuff like that that could get you through a hard day, not to mention he was an outstanding Doc.

February 27th I was sitting around in our hooch waiting for our nighttime flight. Disney and I had run together earlier in the day. I finally felt like I was getting back into shape. I was scheduled to fly from 0200 to 0600 with an Air Force pilot. As I stood looking around, I contemplated how different it was being with the wing instead of with my platoon. My responsibilities never ended when I was a grunt platoon commander. There was always something to do. I was either planning an ambush/patrol, going on an ambush/patrol, worrying about my men and what they needed or doing paperwork for command. Boots were always a concern and I had to make sure my troops' feet were in good shape. I didn't have any of these responsibilities as an AO and my only real concern was to take care of myself, the plane I flew and the men on the ground we were supporting.

I ran into Pappy Flynn later. He was heading to some club in Da Nang. He started talking about stocks and how it had become his new preoccupation. Which worked out well for me when we ended up making money in silver futures that Chastain had arranged to buy through a contact of his in New York.

On the second night we just drank through all the chaos. All I knew at that point was my R and R to Australia had come through, and I was heading out on March 1st to let it all hang out.

Australia was absolutely amazing, and boy did I really need that break to recharge. Coming back was hard but fuck it, I had a great time. I hooked up with a guy from my Basic class, Bill Brignon and we hung around together on R and R. Met a couple of girls at Bondi Beach the first day.

Bill and I grabbed a cooler of beer and headed down to the beach where we met the girls. I did a low crawl up to them which made them laugh. We took them out on a double date later to the Bourbon and Beefsteak had way too much to eat and drink.

The real problem with Sydney though, was it rained five out of the six days I was there, and it really cut into my beach hustle specialty. On the fourth night in Australia, I went back to the Bourbon and Beefsteak and met a beautiful blonde. She had come in with her friend and been seated at the corner table. I bribed the Maître D to sit me next to her and after a while I had a conversation going. I guess my words worked because she invited me to a dinner party the next night at her place. I told her I would go but only if she had lunch with me the next day.

The next day I met her where she worked as a secretary for three guys who were at the racetrack for the day. Lunch was champagne and curry and we had a local newspaper guy take our photo which was published in the next day's paper.

It was a festive party that night. Bill and I brought six bottles of champagne and would have brought more if we had more hands to carry it all. Di was a fantastic hostess and really knew how to work a room as well as a stove. She was a great dancer and we burned some calories dancing that night.

She was the first truly feminine woman I had been with in a long time. Long blonde hair, hazel green eyes, a perky little nose, the softest lips ever. After everyone left, I slept with her for a couple of hours until her roommate came home and then went back to the hotel.

The next day I met her for lunch and more champagne then picked her up at 7pm for dinner. We had drinks first at Bourbon and Beefsteak and then German food and dancing at Rhein Schloss. More champagne flowed and more pictures were taken and after a lot of drinks and a good effort on my part we finally made love. The phone rang at 5am and that was it for me in Australia. I had to shower and get my uniform together. She made me some crackers and cheese while I was getting my gear together and I wolfed them down with a beer chaser. I couldn't kiss her enough and I honestly felt like I was in love with her after just two days. I asked her how that was even possible as the cab pulled up and honked. She kissed me goodbye and I left with a heavy heart promising to come back to her as soon as possible.

Once I got back from Australia, I started flying a lot. I tried to keep a journal while I was in Vietnam, which we were ordered not to do of course but many of us knew the historical significance of what was going on and kept them anyway. Honestly, I was so busy flying missions at this point I neglected my journal and focused more on staying alive.

On March 16th I got the chance to support my old battalion in an operation named WORTH. It was around Happy Valley just below Charlie ridge, so I knew the area well. I had called in my first air strike there when I spotted 17 VC on patrol and killed them all with a direct Napalm strike. I knew the officers on the ground that I was talking with and it really helped a lot to coordinate and run the airstrikes and artillery.

I got to talk to Capt. Ripplemeyer Charlie company commander, Pete Ruane a former FO with Delta Company who was now the battery commander for Golf battery and Capt. Witney who was now with the 1/4 all in the open. Not having to use call signs or codes since we all knew each other's voices let us proceed with support for the ground troops with no delays. I am pretty sure we were only 3 or 4 hundred feet above the ridgeline for our entire flight. Delta took a lot of casualties that day and I could see many of them from my aerial position. I was literally watching my friends die before my eyes. 1/7 got the best support possible from us that day but a lot of good men died. I am not really sure why the NVA didn't shoot at us since we were skimming along at such a low altitude. Just had to chalk that one up to luck, I guess.

The day prior Delta Company took a crap load of casualties and a CH46 medevac helicopter got shot down right under me. That was one that really devastated me, seeing a CH-

46 medevac get hit with an RPG as it was about 100 feet up with a full load of wounded and flight crew was almost too much to believe. Four wounded Marines burned alive in the crash. Everyone else got out because the pilot was savvy enough to auto rotate to the ground and land without breaking up completely. That was one of the parts of the job that sucked the most, there is nothing you can do but watch your fellow brothers in arms die. I can't imagine a worse death.

Not surprisingly I got drunker than hell that night, which just happened to be the day before St. Pat's Day. Of course, the next morning Flynn, Coleman and I got up, still drunk of course, and serenaded everyone with "When Irish Eyes Are Smiling". St. Patrick's Day aside, it was not lost on me that the more I saw death in this war the more I drank. I did have my Australian girlfriend now though and thoughts of her helped me cope a little better. I had written to her a few times since I had gotten back and even sent her a new pair of pearl earrings to replace the ones, I broke the last night I was in Australia.

I got shot at by a .50 caliber machine gun one night and boy did it really have us hoping to get out of there. Mostly because the idiot Air Force pilot I was flying with had flown us down some place we had no business going at night. We flew without lights of course but you could still easily track the plane on the ground by the illumination from engine sparks and the sound of the engine. I could see the tracer rounds tracking our O-1 and was screaming at the pilot to get us the hell out of there. He did the best he could at 85 mph.

This was the first time in a while that I was really concerned about flying and all I really wanted to do was get on flat ground, but I was trapped 500 feet in the air. The incident really forced me to come to terms with what would happen if we were shot down though and although I was no longer afraid of getting shot down. Honestly it seemed like as good a way to go as any and it would be a quick death. I was resolved however that I would not be captured on any terms by the VC or NVA and would die in the fight before surrender. That was the reason I always carried an extra .45 round in my upper left pocket as a last resort before capture.

March of 68 seemed to go a little faster than most months which was a good thing. I got lucky enough to catch a C-130 to Ubon Ratchathani, Thailand on the 19th with an AO Warrant Officer friend of mine named Bill. Because of the rocket attacks almost every night they would fly all the C130's out each night and bring them back every morning to prevent them from being damaged. The flight only took an hour and a half and as we landed, we knew the Air Force once again had it made. Instead of a defensive perimeter, the first thing we saw was the bowling alley. Laughing, and promising to be back at dawn the next morning to the pilots on the aircraft, we grabbed a bottle of whiskey from the O Club, departed the airbase by taxi and got a hotel room in town.

It was a great night to say the least. We decided to have dinner. My first taste of Thai food ever and it was fantastic, but so spicy I couldn't finish the whole meal! I got two baths complete with massages. Ate a surprisingly good steak dinner at the Lotus Café and then took the gal home from the Tokyo Bath House. She was a hot little number that gave a tremendous massage and man was she good in the sack. It was always funny to me that in Vietnam they call sex Boom-Boom and in Thailand Pompom. Bill woke me up at 0430 and we rushed back to the flight line in such a hurry I had to put my clothes on in the taxi. Luckily, we got there just in time to catch the C-130 heading back to Marble Mountain as it taxied down the runway. We ran in front of the plane and waved our arms wildly, the plane shrieked to a halt and they pulled us up through the hatch underneath the aircraft. I immediately fell asleep on the floor of the plane.

When I got back, I was still drunk from the night before, so I slept all day and got up and flew all night. It was only then that I realized I left in such a hurry I forgot to leave any money for the beautiful woman I had spent the night with. I'm still sorry about that one, she was very nice and took great care of me.

Like I said, March flew by and before I knew it April was on me. I was just over three months away from getting out of this damn war, but I was determined not to let that thought affect my actions as a Marine. I still had a job to do and I was going to do it all the way just like I had every day since I got here. It helped though that

I got to spend the last week of March as duty AO at Division. It was a dull week with no flying, but it was also a full week of not getting shot at and I was grateful for the break.

I was cautiously optimistic heading into April, but every ounce of that optimism ran out the door when I heard that Frank O'Brien had been killed in Operation Worth. I was having breakfast with Murphy and we found out as we were coming out of the chow hall. It hit me hard I must admit, and I regretted never writing him a letter while I was in Vietnam immediately. The worst part of that awful news was that the operation ended the day after Frank was killed and he had orders waiting at Battalion to send him on R and R duty to Taipei for two months. What a rotten shame the whole deal was.

When there were up times in Vietnam you could usually count the minutes until there was news that would bring you down but the same was usually true in reverse and when the down times came it seemed easier to find something that you could cling to that would bring you back up, no matter how small. The news of Frank's death was hard to deal with, but I was still clinging to my fascination with Diane. She had sent a nice letter finally with a few photos and some info on her working in the United States. Pop helped me lock up my orders to MCRD San Diego and I knew if I could just make it through the next hundred days that she would come out in October to the States and life would be great. Of course, I still had a bevy of beauties that I had to check out waiting for me to get back to the good old US of A. Man was it ever going to be a field day. Like I said there was always an up when something got you down and was that prospect ever an up.

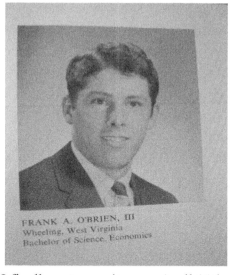

FRANK A. O'BRIEN, III
Wheeling, West Virginia
Bachelor of Science, Economics

I finally got my wings on April 11th and had over one hundred and fifty combat hours

337

as an AO. I was flying hops left and right at this point and working lots of air control as they kept sending more and more flights to us. We were bombing south of the Hoyan river mostly at that point and word was we were killing a lot of civilians. That thought bothered me somewhat. I never wanted to kill anyone who was just trying to innocently make it through the damn war. But in this damn war, who was to say who was an innocent civilian and who wasn't? There was just no way to sort it out because the enemy used the locals as a sort of shield by stocking arms and supplies in their villages and conscripting their men to fight whether they wanted to or not. They cooperated with the V.C. and thus aided them but honestly, they were just victims of the circumstances. Which sure cost a lot of good Marines their lives without question.

It was really something, though to hold the power of life and death over people as you fly over them. With the flick of a switch and a few words I could call in fire power that was nothing less than apocalyptic to the people below and amazing in its awe from the air. We had air and artillery at our beck and call, and it was daunting sometimes. It was a power I didn't like, a power that I struggled with daily and a power I never hope to have again. War was without question in my mind the ugliest thing a man could encounter, and I prayed daily that when my tour was up, I would never have to kill again. But as much as I hated the power that I had to unleash almost daily and the lives that it cost I knew that it had to be done.

Stayed at Phu Bai on April 25th. I had been flying with Task Force X-Ray for the past week. We helped a recon team "Fudge Cake" out of a really tight spot yesterday. They were surrounded by V.C. and we guided them by radio to a nearby LZ, that was really just a bomb crater, then called in the Huey's and a 46 to extract them. It seemed like it took forever because they were dragging their KIA and several wounded with them as they shot their way through the dense jungle terrain! I could hear the firefight in the background as I talked to them on the radio. We marked the enemy with our rockets and the Huey gunships lit them up placing incredibly accurate fire on target as the troops moved toward the extraction point.

The 46 pilot was top notch and the Huey's really gave him the close support he needed while he hovered for a full fifteen minutes to pull the entire team out. We got to see them again for a few minutes in Phu Bai while they dropped off their wounded. They were ragged and beaten. So exhausted they could barely talk and seemed just utterly done at the moment , but still they gave us thanks for getting them out of a shit situation. It was never clearer to me than that day that was the reason I was there. Those men were alive because we did our job, and it was a good feeling inside knowing we had helped them out and it is one of my better recollections I have to this day.

I should add that when Cpt. R. Johnson flew together on the day of the Recon Tm. Extraction, this was only the 2d time we had ever flown together, and he was new as I recall. He told me at the end of the flight that he was going to put me in for a Silver Star and I should put him in for a DFC. I was slightly taken aback, and I told him no, as we were just doing our jobs. In retrospect today, I have thought about putting him in for a DFC, as pilots almost never got recognized by the ground for what they did in the air. He did an outstanding job in flying the plane that day and he did what I told him to do as crazy as it sounds: a Lieutenant telling a Captain what to do. But that was the way it was between the Marine AO's and the Army pilots!

I spent that night in Phu Bai since they always needed an AO up there first thing in the morning. I remember they had a big tent the Army had rigged up to serve as an Officer's club. You could always tell who the Marines were from the Army guys in the dimly lit (literally by lantern) tent because the Marines would be up at the bar drinking and the Army types would be sitting, writing letters, playing cards and once I swear, I even saw one crocheting!

Of course, in the odd balance of the war the next day we narrowly missed getting shot down by an A-4 who fired his rockets late pulling out of a rocket marking run. The Phu Bai area was difficult to control fixed wing air in. The ceiling was low at the time and it greatly increased the danger of midair collisions. So, occasionally you would get a pilot on station who was new, anxious or close to bingo fuel and he would not wait for me to tell him what to do. The scenario was supposed to go like this: Once the enemy was marked by our rockets, or by my hand-held smoke dropping out of the cockpit if we were out of rockets. I would ask Dash 1 (the lead pilot) if he had the target in sight. I would then brief him (if I had not already done so) on the azimuth heading he was to fly, verify that he knew where any friendlies were, and then he would start his run on the target. When I felt he was in the right direction toward the target I would say "cleared hot" and then, and only then, was the pilot supposed to release his ordinance.

For Dash 2 if the bombs of Dash on were, let's say 25 meters south of the target. I would tell Dash 2: Do you have Dash 1's bomb drop in sight? He would say yes, and then I would tell him to drop 25 meters north of Dash 1's drop. If he had that insight, I would clear him hot on his run if he looked good to me. The experienced fixed wing pilots were well aware of the routine since it also protected the ground troops from an accidental bombing! My biggest nightmare, and I would say it was true for all of us AO's, was to kill Marines because someone made a mistake.

We went to great pains to avoid any danger to the troops on the ground. In fact, more than once I had to call off a pilot who was in an actual bomb run because I did not feel comfortable that he had the proper target in sight. I could always bring them around again for another run and make sure he had the right target in sight. Many times, I had to caution pilots about dropping too low because their bombs weren't arming in time and would dud. The 250 pounders and the napalm bombs all had a fuse device on them so they would not arm to explode until the pilot could safely get away. In other words, if the pilot came in too low the bomb just wouldn't be in the air long enough to arm and all you got was an unexploded bomb on the ground that was more harm than help to the ground troops. Always seemed to me that the Marine pilots were much better than the Air Force pilots when it came to close air ground support. So, I guess you could say we were happiest when we were working with Marines in the air and on the ground. Even then it was never far from my mind that life was fragile and always in the balance .

We had been flying so much that time was passing faster than ever it seemed. Before I knew it, May was upon me and I had less than seventy days to go in country. May 5th, we ran three flights of fixed wing flights for 1st Battalion 27th Marines. Those A-4's using Delta 2's are hard to pick up at first because of their high dive and high drop. So, we had to make sure they were dropping high enough they could climb out in time.

Flying up to the northern TAOR was a real pain in the ass. The real issue with going up north though was the weather. It was always bad which meant we had to fly low so we could do our job right. That made us incredibly susceptible to small arms fire and of course counting down the days that sort of risk was a lot for me to take on mentally. We tried to always fly "feet wet" (low and over the ocean) when flying between Marble Mountain and Phu Bai so we didn't have to fly over the bad guys and risk getting shot down. On May 6 we almost had a midair collision with a Bird Dog that was flying up to replace us. Both aircraft were at about 5000 feet and we were not very attentive. I happened to glance up from the map I was reading and I saw the other Bird Dog headed straight for us. I yelled into the intercom "Dive Dive" which the pilot did immediately and we barely missed each other. The pilot and I and the pilot in the other aircraft talked excitedly about our narrow escape from disaster and how we had to pay more attention in the future. The old adage that most midair collisions occur on a clear day applied to this incident. It was routine for us to travel the route the same way every day. I breathed a sigh of relief realizing how close to death we came through our own carelessness.

We had a farewell party for Thatch that night and it was a wild time. Everyone was dancing around the hooch like wild men to the tape recorder, drunk off our asses. We put Thatch on the Medi-Vac copter over to the terminal, passed out drunk with a note on his chest explaining who he was and where he was heading....Home! What a way to leave Nam!

After that, I spent the next few nights drying out. I had been drinking too much at the time trying to push away the loneliness that set in at night. There was nothing really for us to do at night except drink or try to watch a movie at the club. But the film would always break at least once during the movie and it would be a long pause before it was spliced back together and playing again. Sometimes I was just plain worried from the day's flights and needed to relieve the tension with a few cold ones. I wasn't as concerned as I had been when I started off as an AO because I had come to know my in-flight capabilities more and I trusted myself to make the right calls. But the idea of going down was always in the back of my mind. With just 68 more days to go I was starting to get a little more nervous that what had happened to Frank O'Brien might happen to me. It was not that uncommon and was a thought you couldn't really avoid.

CHAPTER 23
SHORT TIMER

In mid-May I was lucky enough to get sent to the Philippines for Escape and Evasion School. It was a required school for all AO's and pilots. So, even though I had been in Vietnam for months, I was still required to go to E&E school, and I was looking forward to the break to tell the truth. It was a solid school and a pretty good time overall.

I flew into the Philippines on a Marine C130 and landed in Subic Bay. We were taken to a BOQ area where we were put up until we went to school in two days. I met a group of mostly Navy pilots who were also going to E&E school and we made plans to meet up together later in Olongapo at the 123 Club.

I contacted my old Sigma Chi fraternity brother from San Diego State Rick Lowery and his wife Kathy in Subic Bay as soon as I could and had dinner at their house. The dinner was great, and it was good to see Rick again, but I couldn't wait to get back and link up with my new pilot buddies and go to the 123 Club. Rick gave me a ride to the club and warned me about not violating curfew.

The club was loud, the music great, and the women were beautiful, and all spoke English. As I recall, there was a hotel in the back of the bar where there were a bunch of girls and we each picked one out for the night to go to bed with. We all left the next morning to walk back to the base because we could not go back after midnight due to the curfew.

I joined back up with the pilots and we went back over the bridge to enter the base. A group of young Filipino boys were swimming in the river below asking for money which we threw down to them as we passed overhead.

We started school the next day and it was a joke for me but a real process for the pilots. I almost missed the first day and really didn't get much out of it because I was working on about an hour's sleep. It was all I could do just to stay awake. It was interesting during the day when the local Filipino indigenous people taught us how to eat off the land which I found interesting, especially the fishing part. But at night the pilots were afraid to lay down on the ground and sleep. I just rolled up in my poncho and went to sleep. They were all very concerned about snakes and other varmints but after 6 months as a grunt in Vietnam that wasn't a problem for me much to their amazement.

Most of them stayed up, both nights! But overall, the school was good, and I learned some valuable tactics to utilize in the event that we got shot down. I was still determined that if that ever did happen, I would not be taken captive alive. The stories of the POW's here are too brutal and I don't want to suffer that kind of pain and indignity.

I would be remiss in my tale if I failed to mention Kadena Air Force Base at this point. I had the pleasure of spending one night there before my return. It was like living in Heaven for a day to a Marine in Vietnam. "Hold On I'm Coming" by Sam & Dave was the song playing as I took in the view. You see Kadena was where all the stewardesses from

America stayed the night before they went back on their return flights to America. It just so happened that I ran into a bunch of A-6 pilots that just all happened to have mechanical failures in their planes that day. A strange coincidence for sure but you have to keep your equipment in top order to fight a war. Needless to say, that day was amazing and just what I needed before heading back.

I got back from Escape and Evasion school on the 20th of May 1968 and we are still flying a lot of missions out of Phu Bai. The only thing I got from sleeping in that jungle was a sore tailbone. It was increasingly boring staying in that bunker. There were just too many "heavies" and not enough hell raisers.

Barksdale was there though, and we would tie one on from time to time. We snuck out to the Stone Elephant or MAG 11 when we could. I heard that another friend from back home Johnny Callahan had been killed but my folks had yet to write to me about it at this point, so I just figured it was a rumor until I really knew. I felt really bad about it anyway, after all we had known each other practically since birth and I was really close to his parents Betty and Red. All I could think was, if it was true, it would be hard to go home and face them.   Overall, May wasn't a bad month aside from the news about Johnny . John Low had also written and told me that he had made me over $1000 in the stock market, which at the time was quite a bit of money. And our Benchmark account in silver futures under Chastant's guidance had gone up 125%. So, I knew that when I got back, I would be set financially.

As a treat for myself I wrote to Rick Lowery and asked him to order me a handmade wooden bar from a craftsman he knew locally and also put the order in for my new MG. I planned to buy all new stereo gear on the way home in Okinawa. Now all I had to do was get myself home in one piece.

June wasn't quite the month May had turned out to be. We did a lot of drinking that month. The going away party for Major Wanner was crazy and we all stayed up until 2 am just drinking in our hooch with almost our entire unit in attendance and totally wrecked the place. A table full of drinks and popcorn all over the floor. If I was a cockroach this would be heaven to me. We had also been flying quite a bit which always made the time go faster, although now we were getting shot at regularly, which sucked but I was so short by that time and nothing really pissed me off anymore.

The worst part about June by far though was that the Division implemented a new policy against two R&R's so it didn't look like I would get back to Australia but if I could somehow scrounge up some orders LaRocca had me on a stand-by seat. It was a stressful month, but I was dealing with it well and doing a lot of running on the beach to try and keep in shape and combat all the partying we had been doing.

With the coming of July, I was just 14 days away from getting out of Vietnam, and par for the course, on July 6th just eight days out we took two rocket hits close to the club during a big show and had to evacuate. Despite the fact that the rockets were landing closer and closer to the club, nobody left until there was a very loud explosion outside. Then, we all grabbed our drinks and ran for the bunkers. I will always remember someone yelling out for a "six pack to go" and we ran and dove head-first into the bunkers just in time to avoid the last rocket hit very close to the club. The next day I was amazed that none of us had been killed or injured when I saw how close the rocket had come to the club and the damage it had caused, I grew pensive and reflected on the whole year and realized how lucky I had been.

Thinking about all the things that had happened and all the things that could have happened since I got here almost a year ago, I had no right to complain. I just wanted to be around women again. You have to be a man among other men with no women around to truly appreciate the value and importance of women. They really are a precious gift from God.

On July 7th, 1968 I flew my last hop and
I can tell you I was a little on edge. I didn't
want to make it this far and get shot down on
my last flight after so many close calls along
the way. By the end of my time as an AO all
but three Marine 0-1's had been shot down.
The remaining three oddly were ones that
patrolled up near the DMZ. It was thankfully
an uneventful hop and we returned safely to
Marble Mountain without issue.

I was working out as much as I could to
try and get back into shape before heading
back to my golden sand beaches of San
Diego and working my magic, but it was hard
with all the drinking and the heat was almost

355

unbearable. I got to spend two days in Ubon on the 8th – 10th and it was a good last look at Thailand and the amazing girls up there. Then on July 13th I packed my gear for the big flight home.

I was now the salty war vet who was dirty, grubby and tan and when we got on the plane it was like reliving history from the other side as the fresh-faced Marines passed us in their clean new pressed uniforms with glints of home still in their eyes. Good luck Devil Dogs. Goodbye Vietnam.

CHAPTER 24
HOME AGAIN,
HOME AGAIN!

When the wheels of the plane touched down in California it was as if the weight of the world came off my shoulders. I was free to do as I pleased and didn't have to run into the middle of a fire fight or reign death from above. But at the same time, it was somehow a foreign place to me coming home after so long away in a place where you were on alert all day every day. It was going to take some adjusting to feel comfortable again in the real world.

Luckily, I had a fantastic network of family and friends that could help me adjust and a list of women that I wanted to play the field with. California had plenty of beauties for me and plenty of cold beer to drink.

Pop was proud of the way I handled myself in Vietnam and it made me feel great to have his respect. Mom cried when she saw me of course, tears of joy, she said but most likely tears of relief if you asked me. She no longer had to stay up and worry if I was alive at night.

I spent a lot of time drinking cold beer and chasing women in the months after I got home, and it was fantastic. My orders to MCRD originally assigned me to the RTR. After talking to other lieutenants assigned to RTR I decided I didn't want to be assigned to RTR because, I was informed that I would be spying on the DIs to help enforce new rules about harassment of recruits. I went to the legal office on board base and told Maj Zieman that I was a lawyer, and he was dumbfounded. He jumped up and said he was going to have my orders changed, which he subsequently did, and I was assigned to the Staff Judge Advocate's office at Marine Corps Recruit Depot, San Diego where I served as both a defense attorney and a prosecutor. I met another lawyer in the office, a Captain Bill McAdam who had actually served as a company commander in Vietnam and we became fast friends. I ended up separating from active duty in March of 1970, as did Bill, and we started a law firm called McAdam and Neil.

I settled down enough to get to work on my legal career and started a firm with Bill who would be my partner for the next two years before we parted ways and I went on to the firm of Holt Rhoades & Hollywood. The firm that would eventually become the senior partner in ,and where I would spend most of my professional life as a lawyer.

About a month after I got back from Vietnam, I received a letter from Rod Chastant. It contained a check in the amount of $500, payable to me. It was the balance owed me from our silver investment account. In the letter, he told me that Mike Hendrickson had been shot down and killed. I didn't realize at the time that I was reading the letter that Rod was also dead. Both AOs who had extended were KIA. It seemed it was a blessing that Disney, Coleman and I had torn up our papers to extend.

Anyone who watched the news could see that the veterans returning home, in most of the country, were being treated like criminals. Most people who had no connection to the war or had not been themselves would watch reports on the news and had decided we were all evil men who killed women and children at will and raped everything in sight. The truth of the matter was mistakes were made and dramatized by the news to the point it made us the enemy in our own country.

I was lucky. San Diego was a largely military town, so the anti-war sentiment wasn't too bad, although it was still present. In other places you would hear stories of soldiers being spit on, yelled at and even beaten. The real shame is these were men that were asked to lay down their lives for their country. Men who had to go to a place where they lived with the possibility of being killed in the most horrific ways every single second of every single day. No matter if they were in a field combat unit on patrol, in the air as an AO or just on liberty at a bar having a drink. Death was a constant companion in Vietnam, and it could come at any place at any time. Many of these men were also young and many drafted to serve. They did not have the experience in life or combat to tell the difference between enemy and friend in a foreign land under heavy fire. They lacked the impulse control of a man of age and just couldn't process the magnitude of what was going on around them.

We must also remember that in war you have no choice but to demonize your enemy as a soldier. If you don't force yourself to have some sort of anger toward them, it becomes difficult to pull the trigger when the time comes, and it could cost you your life. It is a horrible but undeniable part of the reality of war. A reality that most will never know thank the Lord but a reality, nonetheless.

So, while you sit in your American coffee shop enjoying the air conditioning, hot coffee and freshly made sandwich these are the men that you must thank for that freedom. The war in Vietnam was largely unpopular and believe me when I tell you the Marines, I served with didn't like it either but most felt that they had a duty to their country to follow the orders given them and a duty to those they loved back home to return alive.

It is easy to concede the fact that many mistakes were made in the way the war in Vietnam was fought and I would never argue that point about Vietnam or any other war for that fact. War is awful from every angle and there is no such thing as a good war but many times they are necessary to protect those who cannot protect themselves and Marines will always stand and fight for those who cannot. We are the sharp edge of the sword that must exist, so everyone has an opportunity to share that freedom. The Marines and Soldiers that I served with in Vietnam were never given the welcome home that they deserved and only in the last few decades have they been given help to process and handle the issues they deal with every day arising from the war both physical and mental. You see the most horrific part of war is that when it is over the death toll still rises. Combatants and non-combatants alike suffer from physical and mental conditions that lead often to death and many times to death by their own hand. So, if I would ask anything of the readers of this book it would be this one small thing. If you see a Vietnam Veteran go up to them, shake their hand and say, "WELCOME HOME", the one thing we never really got.

I lost many friends to suicide and the effects of Agent Orange over the coming years and it weighed heavily on me every day along with my own special demons I had to deal with. Thankfully I had my family, friends and community for support and while I had my moments for the most part life was pretty good.

After my separation in March of 1970, I admit that I missed the Corps. It offered a level of service to one's country and a spirit of comradery you just don't find anywhere else in the world. Although in 1971 my world would change forever, and I would find the one person that I would be able to share my world with.

I first saw Jan in Mexico when I was down on a trip with friends. We of course were drunk and rowdy and completely ignored by Jan and her friends, but I couldn't get her face out of my mind. As luck would have it, we would run into each other on an elevator in San Diego a few weeks later and she would agree to meet me after her class was over. We met that night at Bully's where I asked her what she wanted to drink. She said a coke, as she was only 19. We were married six months later!

I missed the Corps and still had a sense of duty to my county.
Something I think never really goes away in most Marines. So, in the summer of 1973 I joined the Marine Corps reserves. Over the next several years I would attend many Marine reserve schools and was a member of various reserve units.

In the early 1980's after bouncing around from here to there I was assigned to an extended active-duty position as the Executive Officer of the Exercise Control Group for operations Freedom Pennant I and II. The Marine Corps had started working closely with Australian forces to plan a series of amphibious landings in western Australia near Perth. I was sent a letter by Marine Corps HQ asking that I return to the full-time reserves to help with command coordination of the operation. The operation went beyond expectations and has been a training exercise between the two countries ever since.

In 1983 I went back to the reserves and took command of the 4th Tank Battalion in San Diego. even though I had not been a Tanker. I was told that I was selected for my leadership abilities.

Jan and I had been together for a little over 12 years at that point and even though there were points during that first year we both thought we might throw in the towel. It was a lot of adjusting for both of us in the beginning. I was not used to living with anyone and was quite gruff if I do say so myself. Jan was young and I am sure living with a Marine still dealing with the war was no easy task. But somehow, we made it through those early days and now had not only each other to worry about but our two children Megan and Sean.

After 4th Tanks I transitioned to the 1st Marine Expeditionary Force Reserve Augmentation Unit as the Assistant G-3 for Plans. Now a full bird colonel, I participated as Commanding General, during war games, including the annual Global War Games in Newport, RI.

In 1989, I was promoted to the rank of Brigadier General in the Marine Corps Reserve. I, along with Jan, attended a school in Washington DC along with my active-duty counterparts. The school was known as "The Charm School " where we were taught how to conduct ourselves as general officers. The week-long school afforded me the opportunity to form close ties with the other 12 newly selected BGs. At the end of the week, I received my assignment. I would be the backup general Boomer at Camp Pendleton in the event of war. Saddam Hussein, as it turned out. Made this a reality.

On Sept 4th, 1990 I received a telephone at 1500 from Major General Sheehan at Headquarters Marine Corps, Washington D.C., asking me if I was ready to come on active duty and assume command of Marine Corps Base, Camp Pendleton. It did not come as a surprise as I had been in contact with Headquarters Marine Corps several times over the past few weeks. I told him I was ready to take command and requested two days to get my affairs in order and report. It was a difficult decision to make heading back to war, but I had a duty to my country and to my fellow Marines to help in any way I could. My orders came through with the effective date of Sept 7, 1990.

The next few days were a bit chaotic trying to structure work, trials, clients and family obligations while I would be serving on active duty. This is something many people forget when it comes to our fighting forces. They not only serve our country but have lives to maintain as well. Bills to pay, children to love, businesses to run. Even though we may be at war, life does not stop and the pressure and stress it puts on Marines and their families is immense.

The events of my preparation to take command of Camp Pendleton of course leaked out into what is really a small-town community in San Diego and by midday on the 5th I was being inundated by phone calls from reporters. The Union, LA Times, Channel 10 and several other media outlets both local and national wanted to know more about my being called up to active duty, what that would mean for our community and what effects it would have on the efforts in the Middle East.

I spent most of September 6th with Jan and the kids getting ready for the big day. The local community was making a bit of a deal about me, the local boy taking command of Camp Pendleton. It was all over the radio and TV and the lighthearted jesting helped put me at ease. Knowing that not only was my family but my community behind me in my decision helped me a lot.

The funniest part to me during the entire process was Jan and her honest reaction to the news. I had been spending the day with my son Sean and he had overheard me telling some colleagues of my plan and agreed not to tell anyone in the family until I could break the news. So of course, when we got home that evening, he was understandably excited and simultaneously put off when I did not break the news to his mother right away.

I eventually told Jan and her first response was "That's okay we can just reschedule the trip to Hawaii in November". Then she gave me a kiss like only she could. It was so much like her and such a huge part of why I love her so deeply. She was of course half serious but mostly trying to break the tension of the situation with a bit of humor and I think the entire family needed it at the time. Megan and Sean were both excited and proud of their father but at the same time relieved when they learned I would not be going to Saudi Arabia and therefore would be out of physical danger for the most part.

The community both business and personal gave me all the support I needed. The press coverage was a nice pat on the back for a lifetime local and the lawyers and judges that I worked with every day agreed for the most part to continue my cases until I returned to my civilian life.

Having covered all the bases as it was, both personally and professionally and with the support of my family and community I reported to Camp Pendleton on September 7th, 1990. My first stop was not my office or the headquarters building at all but the flag post that overlooks the gates of Camp Pendleton. I parked my car and walked to the base of the flag, where I stared at those stars and stripes that represent so much to myself and all true Americans. I took a moment and knelt in prayer for our troops already in place overseas and the many I knew would follow if things kept heading the direction they were heading. I prayed that God would give me the strength to command these men and that it would not be the same kind of war that I had known, especially for the Marines on their return home.

War is something I knew my Marines would be able to deal with but coming home to a nation that hates you for doing what you in your heart of hearts only believed was your duty to self and country. You do what you have to do sometimes just to stay alive. Coming home to that scorn resentment was worse than any battle you could ever fight in a war. I prayed that I would be able to use my position in the community to help the returning Marines to be able to avoid the same fate my fellow Marines and I suffered on our return home from Vietnam. We never got our welcome home and I'll be damned if I would let that happen to them.

One of my duties during the Desert Storm/Desert Shield action would be to prep and train Marines for combat as it was during any war. Marines called up from reserve units, fresh recruits from boot camp and salty dogs that hadn't seen combat in a while all needed to be refreshed and know that the command was always behind them. We did readiness exercises in case of attack and trained extensively for NBC type attacks since Hussein was known for using this tactic and would most likely resort to it in case of all-out war. There were also endless meetings, paperwork, logistical, pay, and dependent issues as well as numerous other tasks that needed attention daily. It was hard on my family, but they stood by me strong every day. I made it a point to visit the schools and talk to the dependents left behind, which was admittedly difficult, but their morale appeared for the most part to be high throughout. The local community was great about helping with donations especially around Christmas time.

It was a particularly sad reoccurring thought I had during this time that really seemed to haunt me most. It seemed that with the fall of the Berlin wall not so far in the past that our world was looking at an unprecedented period of peace right in the eye. Yet here we were again with our American fighting forces staring straight down the barrel of another war and the possibility of thousands of soldiers and marines dying again in a far-off place longing for home. I was confident however that we were right in our actions and standing for the world in a statement saying essentially that bullies will not be tolerated on the world stage.

Yes, you could have argued and still can that it was an action motivated by oil price and procurement but beyond that argument at its base you had a man who devalued human life to the point of NBC attacks and invasion of a sovereign nation for his own financial gain and megalomaniacal agenda. That is something that should never be tolerated no matter what business interests happen to be involved in the background.

As the U.N. deadline of January 15th, 1990 approached, I had become increasingly concerned with base security and increased our threat level to THREATCON ALPHA at all gates. I was also concerned with my own personal security and that of my family. We were without question at this point going to war and we were a good target for any sleeper cells that may be looking to make a statement on American soil. So, I made arrangements for Sean, Megan and Jan to move up to Camp Pendleton and live in the VIP quarters once the shooting started. I also started varying my route of exit from our home and travel to base each day and put the neighbors on notice to look for anything suspicious.

San Diego at the time had the second highest population of Iraqi immigrants in the country, the vast majority of whom were good people and loved their American home. But I knew the second Iraqi bodies started dropping that was highly subject to change. And, as a General in command of Camp Pendleton, with all the publicity I had received and public outreach I had been doing I was a likely target.

With all our worry about the war in Kuwait, as most of you will remember, it was a very well fought war on our behalf. Our Marines, under the command of General Walt Boomer, performed magnificently. We took minimal KIA, WIAs. In total we lost 385 American lives in the war and proceeding action, and while one life is too much, by the standards of war our command did an excellent job of protecting our troops.

To me though the most challenging part about my job during this war was my relationship with the community at large. Not just the press but the everyday Americans from the high-end lawyers I had to deal with in my professional life to the grade school children who wrote letters and gathered supplies to send to our troops. When the whole thing started, I had the same expectations I had when I came home from Vietnam. I was sure there would be rising anti-war sentiment. It would bring back issues that I just didn't want to, nor had the time to, deal with after so many years. I didn't want those brave Marines fighting in Kuwait and Iraq to come back to what we returning Vietnam had to come back to and did my best to make sure that wasn't even an issue. I personally met every group returning, no matter the time or day or night. The community nationwide was very supportive throughout the war. As the troops returned, they were welcomed enthusiastically, for the most part, as heroes. In a sense, it was the welcome home that we had never received when we came home from Vietnam, and I believe provided a lot of closure for Vietnam veterans nationwide. We even had a parade down Broadway in San Diego to celebrate our Desert Storm warriors. I made sure that the Vietnam veterans would

375

march in the parade also. Many of them could be seen visibly crying as people cheered them on.

Those minor protests aside, the community nationwide was very supportive throughout the war and as the troops returned, they were welcomed home as heroes of democracy and treated as warriors fighting for their country. In a sense it was the welcome home that we had never received when we came home from Vietnam and I believe provided a lot of closure for Vietnam Veterans nationwide. I finally felt welcome again in my country more than twenty years after my return.

The memories of those who had died did not escape my thoughts, nor did those who suffered after their return from Vietnam. I noted that I was one of the lucky ones who had a solid support system and wanted to make sure that those returning from this war had all the support they needed.

To that effect I will say this to all of you. No matter your station or status in life if you see a Veteran say hello, say welcome home, say I appreciate what you do for me and mine. Buy them a beer, sit and have lunch with them or tell them a joke. A friendly gesture from the heart can go a long way, it can have deeper meaning than you know and can save a life. It has become increasing PC for people to say, "Thank you for your service" and while most people really do mean it when they say it, most of the time it comes off hollow and very rehearsed, as if said more for the person's own self-gratification than the Veterans well-being.

As far as my time as Commanding General of Camp Pendleton went, I was quite happy to serve my country once again. It would be nine months of service to the day from the time I took over on September 7, 1990 until I was relieved on June 7, 1991. At first it was uncomfortable, as it was unusual for a reserve General to suddenly come in and take over a command like Camp Pendleton, but I was happy to be in the position.

My first staff meeting I sensed that perhaps some of the officers in the room were uncomfortable, for the same reason I was, but I let them know we had one goal, to support our Marines and that my door was always open to discuss anything, at any time. I had a great XO, Col Handlin and an outstanding SgtMaj Robinson and my aide, Dave Morgan. My secretary, Patty, was a huge help as a historian and helping me keep up with current events on the base.

As I grew with the day-to-day responsibilities and duty of my command, I got more comfortable with my situation but still had days where I struggled. Then when time came for me to turn command back over, while a bit sad to give back the base that I had come to love so much. It was nice to go back to things in my civilian life and a normal routine with a newfound bundle of American pride to accompany me along the way.

I wanted to end my musing about my life with a personal note to today's Marines. I pondered quite a while as to what I could say but all I could come back to was Vietnam and how it was so different than the war in Korea and I came to find a simple truth. All wars are different in their own ways so giving anyone advice from that aspect is a bit futile.

So, I will only tell you this Marine...trust your training, and trust your fellow marines, and you will be fine. The Marine Corps does one thing better than anyone. They train you to adapt and overcome in any situation. It will be hard to do at times and you will stumble along the way but when you look back as I do now you want to be able to do so with honor. Safe journeys to you Marines of today and to you Marines of tomorrow. Semper Fi!

CHAPTER 25
FAMILY AND FINAL THOUGHTS

If there is one thing that gives a Marine the will to fight, and the will to survive in those moments that take the greatest courage, it is family. My parents supported my decision to join the Marines. When I came back from Vietnam, I was lucky enough to find the woman who became very supportive of all I would do in my life.

Jan, who was a Canadian, was just 20 when we married, so she had a lot to learn about being a military spouse! Five years into our marriage we had our first child, Megan and a couple of years later, our son, Sean. Our family, like all families, has had some hard times and challenges. But we struggled together through them all.

Active duty and a growing law practice meant I was not always able to be there for our children, but they survived, like most kids. We are now blessed with three grandchildren—Jordan, Michael, and Grace.

CHAPTER 26
IN HONOR OF THE FALLEN

To honor those fallen who never got their "Welcome Home" either, the following is a list of numbers of killed, wounded and missing in action of both Sailors and Marines from 1/7 for the entire year of 1967. I felt it was important to show the number of young lives lost. Lives that never got a chance to really shine but still gave the ultimate sacrifice for our great nation. As well as those like myself that were wounded who still live with the scars of the war both physically and mentally. To all Marines, Sailors, Airmen and Soldiers who never got to hear the words "Welcome Home" from a nation that we loved enough to put our lives on the line for. I have also included a poem written by John Augustine who was part of my OCS class to honor those men I began my journey with. Along with a unit citation and my Navy Cross citation from the night we lost so many including Smedley who himself won the Congressional Medal of Honor.

In closing I would ask this of you reader yet again. As I have said before in this musing of my life history, it is common today when you see a person in the military to say, "Thank you for your service". I'm sure I can speak for most of us and say, thank you for your kindness, it means a lot to know that the people that you fight for have your respect. So, the next time you happen to come across a Vietnam veteran, no matter what branch of service they may be from, shake their hand, tell them thanks for sure but more importantly tell them "Welcome Home" not just for them but for all our veterans from Vietnam who never got to hear those words.

"WELCOME HOME!

THE BOYS OF QUANTICO

From all across the country

They came to join the Corps.

They walked away from everything

Knowing not what was in store.

They pledged their lives & loyalty

For reasons only they would know.

God bless the men who joined back then,

The Boys of Quantico.

In '66 they came 500 strong

384

To find and follow their dreams.

Could they prove they had the stuff

To become an Officer of Marines?

Now some were born to money

While most were regular Joes.

They all faced the test of OCS,

The Boys of Quantico.

They came to test their mettle,

To march & fight & drill.
To push beyond their pain & fear

One clear goal, theirs to fulfill.
Thru sweat & blood they earned

their Bar

And the greatest title one can bestow.

Known as "Marines" 'til Heaven's scenes,

The Boys of Quantico.

At TBS, in classrooms & in the field

For days & nights they trained, you see.

For their mission was to learn to lead

A platoon of Marine Corps infantry.

Their work was hard but each

386

man knew

In the end, to war they would go.

They did their best at TBS,

The Boys of Quantico.

Soon orders came for all of them

To serve their tour in Vietnam.

They'd lead their troops to the fight

In Hue City, An Hoa & Khe Sahn.
They led & loved those in their charge

And bled & died fighting the foe.

One and all, they each stood tall,

The Boys of Quantico.

387

Most came home, though some did not.

All served with honor to behold.

Some were wounded in the flesh,

But all were touched in the soul.

At home they worked to make a life,

To never forget times long ago.

They faced their fear & shed a tear,

The Boys of Quantico.

With years & years of living,

They come to meet again.

They'll laugh & cry with drinks
held high

And they'll remember when

They served with pride and honor

For those who died so long ago.

God bless the men who served
back then,

The Boys of Quantico.

-John Augustine-

Headquarters
1st Battalion 7th Marines
FMP
1st Marine Division
(Rein)
c/o FBO San Francisco,
California 96602

From: Commanding Officer

To: Commanding General, 1st Marine

Division

Via: Commanding Officer, 7th Marines

Subject: Marines Command Chronology for period 010001H to 312400H January 1967.

1. **Designation.** 1st Battalion (Reni), 7th Marines

2. **Period Covered**: 010001H thru 312400H January 1967

3. **Commanding Officers, Executive and Special Staff Officers**

January 1967

Casualties Sustained

4	USMC KIA
0	USN KIA
54	WIA (2 USN)
23	USMC WIA non- med-Evac
10	USMC non-battle

February 1967

Casualties Sustained

2	USMC KIA
1	USN DOW
0	USN WIA
1 5	USMC WIA
1	USN WIA
9	USMC – non-evac
1	USMC – non-battle

0	USN – non-battle

March 1967

Casualties Sustained

4	USMC KIA
0	USMC DOW
30	USMC WIA
0	USN KIA
1	USN WIA
8	USMC WIA Med-

	Evac
4	USMC Non-Battle
0	USN Non-Battle

April 1967

Casualties Sustained

USMC KIA	0
USMC DOW	6
USN KIA	0
USMC WIA	67

USMC WIA non-evac	2
USN WIA	2

May 1967

Casualties Sustained

6	USMC KIA
3	USMC DOW
0	USN KIA
38	USMC WIA
21	USMC WIA non-evac

5	USN WIA
0	USN WIA non-evac
22	USMC non-battle
0	USN non-battle

June 1967

Casualties Sustained

4	USMC KIA
1	USMC DOW
1	USN KIA

51	USMC WIA
26	USMC WIA non-evac
2	USN WIA
1	USN WIA non-evac
3	USMC non-battle
0	USN non-battle

July 1967

<u>Casualties Sustained</u>

7	USMC KIA
3	USMC DOW
0	KIA USN
0	USN DOW
10	USMC WIA
2	USN WIA
13	USMC WIA Non-Evac

0	USN WIA Non-Evac
3	USMC Non-Battle
0	USN Non-Battle

August 1967

Causalities Sustained

7	USMC KIA
3	USMC DOW
0	USN KIA
0	USN DOW

62	USMC WIA
0	USN WIA
42	USMC WIA non-evac
1	USN WIA non-evac

September 1967

Casualties Sustained

1	USMC KIA
3	USMC DOW
0	KIA USN

29	USMC WIA
2	USN WIA
15	USMC WIA Non-Evac
0	USN WIA Non-Evac

October 1967

Casualties Sustained

3	**USMC KIA**

1	USMC DOW
0	KIA USN
14	USMC WIA
0	USN WIA
23	USMC WIA Non-Evac
0	USN WIA Non-Evac
5	USMC Non-Battle
0	USN Non-Battle

0	USMC Dow Non-Battle

November 1967

Casualties Sustained

7	USMC KIA
0	USMC DOW
0	USN KIA
0	USN DOW
26	USMC WIA

December 1967

Casualties Sustained

4	USMC KIA
1	USMC DOW
22	USMC WIA
9	USMC WIANE
3	USN WIANE

Navy Cross

AWARDED FOR ACTIONS

DURING Vietnam War

Service: Marine Corps

Rank: First Lieutenant

Battalion: 1st Battalion

Division: 1st Marine Division

(Rein.) FMF

GENERAL ORDERS:

Authority: Navy Department Board

of Decorations and Medal

CITATION:

407

The President of the United States of America takes pleasure in presenting the Navy Cross to First Lieutenant [then Second Lieutenant] Michael I. Neil (MCSN: 0-101333), United States Marine Corps Reserve, for extraordinary heroism while serving as a Platoon Commander with Company D, First Battalion, Seventh Marines, FIRST Marine Division (Reinforced), Fleet Marine Force, during operations against enemy forces in the

Republic of Vietnam on 20 December 1967. Informed by a squad size ambush patrol that an estimated one hundred Viet Cong were moving toward its position at Phouc Ninh (2), in Quang Nam Province, First Lieutenant Neil quickly organized a twelve-man reaction force and led his small unit to the assistance of the patrol. Disregarding the intense enemy fire, he led his men across 1,300 meters of thickly forested terrain to the Marine patrol which was

heavily engaged with the enemy

force. When the advance was

halted by intense small-arms,

automatic weapons and rifle

grenade fire from the hostile

positions, he, with complete

disregard for his own safety,

exposed himself to the devastating

fire to hurl hand grenades and

direct his men's fire which

momentarily silenced the enemy

weapons. Suddenly, the Marines

came under mortar fire. Shouting

words of encouragement to his

men, he boldly moved through the

hail of enemy fire, leading an

assault against the enemy

positions. Observing a wounded

comrade in an exposed position he

removed his armored vest and

placed it over the casualty to

protect him from further injury.

Picking up the wounded man's M-

79 Grenade Launcher, he delivered

intense and accurate fire against

the enemy. When the momentum of the attack decreased, he rallied his men and led a determined assault into the face of the enemy fire. Throwing hand grenades as he advanced, he destroyed a machine-gun emplacement and mortally wounded several enemies with his pistol. By his bold initiative, gallant fighting spirit and loyal devotion to duty, First Lieutenant Neil reflected great credit upon himself and the Marine Corps and upheld the highest traditions of the

United States Naval Service.

DEPARTMENT OF THE NAVY

HEADQUARTERS UNITED STATES MARINE CORPS
WASHINGTON, D.C. 20380

The Secretary of the Navy takes pleasure in presenting the MERITORIOUS
UNIT COMMENDATION to the:

FIRST PLATOON (-)) REINFORCED
COMPANY D, FIRST BATTALION, SEVENTH MARINES
FIRST MARINE DIVISION (REINFORCED)

for service as set forth in the following:

CITATION:

For exceptionally meritorious service in action in the Republic of Vietnam
on 20 December 1967. Two squad-sized ambush patrols from the First
Platoon (-) (Reinforced), Company D were deployed in the vicinity of
Phuoc Ninh (2) near the entrance to Happy Valley in Quang Nam Province
when a force of 100 North Vietnamese and Viet Cong soldiers carrying
large tubes was observed moving through the area. After notifying the
platoon command post, one squad-sized patrol began moving to engage the
enemy. Simultaneously, reaction forces were deployed from three
directions to blocking positions to prevent the enemy's escape. The platoon
commander and one squad from Company D moving into the area from the
north joined the ambush patrol. Two squads from the east embarked aboard
amphibian tractors from Hill 41. Advancing from the south another squad
engaged the enemy en route. When all elements had reached the objective
area, the platoon commander with five squads searched the area and, after
advancing 400 meters, were attacked from three sides by the hostile force.
Although the enemy moved to within 30 meters of the platoon, the
Marines steadfastly held their positions. A search of the battle area the
following morning revealed numerous enemy casualties and many items of
enemy equipment and weapons, including a lourge amount of rockert
launching equipment and a complete 122mm rocker launcher, were
captured. The seizure of the rocker launcher served to prevent the loss of
lives and valuable government properties of the Free World Armed Forces,

414

...ddition to providing important intelligence information. The defeat of the numerically superior enemy force by the men of the First Platoon (-) (Reinforced), undoubtely saved the Danang vital area from a major attack. Their courage, aggressive fighting spirit and steadfast devotion to duty were in keeping with the highest traditions of the Marine Corps and the United States Naval Service.

All personnel attached to and serving with the First Platoon (-) (Reinforced), Company D, First Battalion, Seventh Marines, First Marine Division (Reinforced) during the above period are hereby authorized to wear the MERITORIOUS UNIT COMMENDATION Ribbon.

For the Secretary of the Navy,

Signed/LEONARD F. CHAPMAN
Commandant of the Marine Corps